PERSPECTIVES ON EARLY CHILDHOOD PSYCHOLOGY AND EDUCATION

SPECIAL FOCUS

Growing Up Poor

Volume 2, Issue 1
Spring 2017

ISBN: 978-1-935625-91-9
ISSN: 2471-1527

Member
Council of Editors of Learned Journals

Special thanks to graduate assistants Kathy Le and Claire Seeger and administrative assistant Gina Cooper for their work on Volume 2, Issue 1.

PERSPECTIVES on EARLY CHILDHOOD PSYCHOLOGY and EDUCATION

TABLE OF CONTENTS

**SPECIAL FOCUS:
GROWING UP POOR**

Editor's Note

Welcome to Volume 2, Issue 1, of *Perspectives on Early Childhood Psychology and Education* (*Perspectives*)! The special focus in this issue is poverty and its negative effects on child development guest edited by Tammy L. Hughes. Readers will find seven manuscripts on this topic plus an introduction to the special focus. One of the seven manuscripts is reproduced from an earlier volume published in 2014 because it is germane to the special focus, authored by leaders in the field, and provides useful information regarding early intervention. In addition, there is one general manuscript addressing the reliability of the Classroom Assessment Scoring System in primary classrooms.

We are preparing the special focus for the fall 2017 issue that will be guest edited by Associate Editor Florence Rubinson. The topic is "Gender diversity: nonconformity and fostering acceptance." Information regarding this special focus is found in the call for papers. We welcome manuscripts for this special focus and manuscripts that contribute to the general section of the issue.

Readers who are interested in becoming a member of the editorial board of *Perspectives* should contact me via email at PECPE@gonzaga.edu or alfonso@gonzaga.edu. In closing I hope you find *Perspectives* to be a useful journal in your research and practice. Please feel free to contact me with ideas, comments, and suggestions. We are very open to innovative ideas and look forward to hearing from you.

Enjoy *Perspectives*!

Vincent C. Alfonso, Ph.D.
Editor

Growing Up Poor

Introduction: Growing Up Poor – The Negative Sequelae on Child Development

Tammy L. Hughes and Taylor Phillips

In 2015, the U.S. Census Bureau reported that nearly 15.5 million children and adolescents in the United States live in families with incomes below the federal poverty threshold. While child poverty rates slightly decreased between 2013 and 2014, the 2016 State of the Union revealed that the United States, in a comparison of its peer countries (e.g., Australia, Canada, Czech Republic, Denmark, Estonia, Finland, France, Germany, Greece, Iceland, Ireland, Italy, Luxembourg, Netherlands, Norway, Poland, Slovak Republic, Slovenia, Spain, and United Kingdom), was an outlier on many measures of inequality. For example, the United States has high levels of income disparity and wealth imbalance, as well as unusually high levels of poverty. Further, the extent of imbalance of inequality the United States can have extremely detrimental effects on one of its most vulnerable subgroups of the population: children.

Child poverty impacts every facet of a child's life (Brooks-Gunn & Duncan, 1997; Petterson & Albers, 2001; Roy & Cybele, 2014; Yoshikawa, Aber, & Beardslee, 2012). Thus, children living in these circumstances draw our attention due to the worrisome negative consequences that can affect short- and long-term child outcomes. It is acknowledged that experiencing poverty during early childhood has a greater impact on certain outcomes, such as cognitive ability and school completion (Bradley & Corwyn, 2002; Sirin, 2005), than does experiencing poverty in later childhood and adolescence. However, exposure to poverty tends to be enduring and resultant problems (e.g., greater risk of physical, cognitive, social, emotional problems, and behavioral problems) also persist into adulthood (Ratcliffe & McKernan, 2012). Efforts to study the impact of poverty, as well as the potential mediating influences of children living in disadvantaged settings, indicate that those children who are exposed to high quality parenting, a greater number and quality of early learning interactions, and high quality educational settings throughout their early lives, can experience positive individual, family, community and society-wide outcomes (Engle & Black, 2008). Therefore, there is a general consensus that it is imperative to invest in supporting quality care for children in the early years of a child's life (Ferguson, Bovaird, & Mueller, 2007). Failing to invest early can lead to detrimental long-term effects for individual children, but also the future of our nation (Samuelsson and Kaga, 2008).

The association between poverty and children's development (e.g., by the age of 2 years old) shows that children from low socioeconomic backgrounds already begin to score lower on standardized tests of intelligence (Anderson, Leventhal, & Dupéré, 2014). These factors often are evident in resource-constrained settings (e.g., crowded living conditions, one income households), when there is a reduction in parental engagement (e.g., familial dysfunction, lack of quality caregiving practices), and/or the unavailability of early learning materials (e.g., lack of participation in quality early childhood programs) (Longtin & Principe, 2016). Importantly, these findings show that while child development is complex and comprises several domains, early development is a strong predictor of later health and productivity leading us to realize that children in the poorest group are in the most need of assistance to reach their full potential.

Summarizing the impact of poverty on child development was noted by the quote "when the stork drops a newborn child into his or her home, the location of that drop has profound implications for the amount of inequality the child will see and experience" (Grusky,Mattingly, & Varner, 2016; p. 5). Researchers confirm this observation; children in the United States are experiencing different socioeconomic conditions very early in the child's developmental period, leading to different developmental trajectories. Diverse schooling conditions also contribute to differential educational outcomes. Ultimately, differences in family socioeconomic status, schooling contexts, and educational outcomes (e.g., test scores) can lead to what is referred to as the income achievement gap. The income achievement gap refers to the difference between test scores of children from high- and low-income families. It is not surprising that a gap exists between children from different socioeconomic backgrounds, but what is surprising is the rate at which the gap reacts to changing conditions. For example, the income achievement gap is very large when children enter kindergarten, but does not widen much between kindergarten and grade 12. That is, with all things being equal, positive school experiences do stabilize early challenges but they do not make up the difference. This shows that quality schooling alone will not offset the impact of poverty conditions on child development (Grusky et al., 2016).

To explain the income achievement gap among students in academic settings, researchers have suggested the income inequality hypothesis (Reardon, 2011). This hypothesis argues that the widening of the achievement gap occurred because the income inequality among families was growing sharply. However, the type of changes that the United States experienced in income inequality do not match the type of changes observed in the achievement gap. For example, as the income inequality gap grew in the 1970s and 1980s due to stagnation at the bottom of the income distribution among families with children, the achievement gap grew mostly as a result of families with children at the top of the income distribution pulling away from their less advantaged peers (Reardon, 2011). This is not to say that income inequality is not responsible for the *academic achievement gap,* but rather that its impact is likely indirect and diffuse. For example, factors such as a weakening social net, inadequate support for families and parents, and increasing segregation of neighborhoods and schools by income, may better explain what is driving this *income achievement gap.* In short, other strong correlations of income inequality such as high rates of teen childbirth, high rates of low birth weight, and high levels of segregation by income among schools are likely contributions to the inequality gap (Caldas, 1999; Chmielewski & Reardon, 2016). Unable to access enriched learning environments, poor children do not have the support to reach their full developmental potential. Lower academic expectations, tracking by ability level and exposure to outdated curricula, are all likely contributors to the achievement gap.

It is well-documented that children need adequate nutrition, families that can provide homes that are financially secure and emotionally stable, and exposure to enriched learning environments to reach their full developmental potential (Brazelton & Greenspan, 2009). What is less clear is how to understand and address the barriers that families living in poverty face. In this special issue authors examine the issues of poverty from a variety of view points including: the impact of homelessness (Battaglia & Reed, this issue); how individuals with autism can access care (Zeleke, Hughes, Tiberi, & Drozda, this issue); indicators of quality preschool programs for children with disruptive behavior disorder symptoms (Brown, McGoey, Graves, & Schreiber, this issue); new initiatives in comprehensive preschool programing for teenage parents (Bagnato, Larson, Miglioretti, Barone-Martin, & McNeal, this issue); as well as the role of the pediatric care (Young-Walker, Stormont, Beucke, & Ell, this issue) and school psychologists in advocating for families (Clarke, Rispoli, Gelbar, Bilias-Lolis, & Bray, this issue). Also in this issue, republished with permission, are recommended interventions for students from low resource environments that have been supported by longitudinal data (Ramey, Sparling, & Ramey, 2014).

Together, the articles in this issue demonstrate the immediate and far-reaching effects of poverty on child development. Given the variety of families in the United States that experience poverty, authors have highlighted the needs of specific populations, assessment considerations and how to determine quality care where evidence-based practices are available. The scope of the complexity surrounding impoverished families suggests that only when school and community personnel are working together in on-going partnerships with families can positive outcomes be realized. A goal of this issue is to provide additional perspectives in the national conversation on what changes are needed to mediate the effect of poverty on early childhood development so as to continue to reduce the size of the achievement gap in the United States.

References

American Academy of Pediatrics Council on Community Pediatrics (2016). Poverty and child health in the United States. *Pediatrics, 137*(4). doi: 10.1542/peds.2016-0339

Anderson, S., Leventhal, T., & Dupéré, V. (2014). Exposure to neighborhood affluence and poverty in childhood and adolescence and academic achievement and behavior. *Applied Developmental Science, 18*(3), 123-138.

Bagnato, Larson, Miglioretti, Barone-Martin & McNeal, this issue

Battaglia & Reed, this issue

Bradley, R. H., & Corwyn, R. F. (2002). Socioeconomic status and child development. *Annual Review of Psychology, 53*(1), 371-399.

Brazelton, T. B., & Greenspan, S. (2009). *The irreducible needs of children: What every child must have to grow, learn, and flourish.* Cambridge, MA: Da Capo Press.

Brooks-Gunn, J., & Duncan, G. (1997). The effects of poverty on child. *The Future of Children, 7*, 55-71.

Brown, McGoey, Graves, & Schreiber, this issue

Caldas, S. J. (1999). Multilevel examination of student, school, and district-level effects on academic achievement. *Journal of Educational Research, 93*(2), 91-100.

Chmielewski, A. K., & Reardon, S.F. (2016). Patterns of cross-national variation in the association between income and academic achievement. AERA Open, 2(3), 1-27.

Clarke, Rispoli, Gelbar, Bilias-Lolis, & Bray, this issue

Engle, P. L., & Black, M. M. (2008). The effect of poverty on child development and educational outcomes. *Annals of the New York Academy of Sciences, 1136*(1), 243-256.

Ferguson, H. B., Bovaird, S., & Mueller, M. P. (2007). The impact of poverty on educational outcomes for children. *Journal of Pediatrics and Child Health, 12*(8), 701-106.

Grusky, D. B., Mattingly, M. J., & Varner, C. E. (2016). State of the union: The poverty and inequality report [Special issue]. *Pathways*, 1-75.

Longtin, S. E., & Principe, G. M. (2016). The relationship between poverty level and urban African American parents' awareness of evidence-based interventions for children with autism spectrum disorders: Preliminary data. *Focus on Autism and Other Developmental Disabilities,* doi:1088357614522293.

Petterson, S. M., & Albers, A. B. (2001). Effects of poverty and maternal depression on early child development. *Child Development, 72*(6), 1794-1813.

Ramey, C. T., Sparling, J. J., & Ramey, S. L. (2014). Interventions for students from low resource environments: The Abecedarian approach. In J. T. Mascolo, V. C. Alfonso, & D. P. Flanagan (Eds.), *Essentials of planning, selecting, and tailoring interventions for unique learners* (pp. 415-448). Hoboken, NJ: John Wiley & Sons.

Ratcliffe, C., & McKernan, S.M. (2012, September). *Child poverty and its lasting consequence: Low-income working families.* (Working Paper No. 21). Washington, DC: The Urban Institute. Retrieved from http://www.urban.org/UploadedPDF/412659-Child-Poverty-and-Its-Lasting-Consequence-Papers.pdf

Reardon, S. F. (2011). The widening academic achievement gap between the rich and the poor: New evidence and possible explanations. In R. Murnane & G. Duncan (Eds.), *Whither opportunity? Rising inequality and the uncertain life chances of low-income children.* New York, NY: Russell Sage Foundation Press.

Roy, A. L., & Cybele, R. C. (2014). Are all risk equal? Early experiences of poverty-related risk and children's functioning. *Journal of Family Psychology, 28*(3), 391-400.

Sirin, S. R. (2005). Socioeconomic status and academic achievement: A meta-analytic review of research. *Review of Educational Research, 75*(3), 417-453.

Samuelsson, I. P., & Kaga, Y. (Eds.). (2008). *The contribution of early childhood education to a sustainable society.* Paris, FR: United Nations Educational, Scientific, and Cultural Organization. (Paris: UNESCO, 2008)

Yoshikawa, H., Aber, J. L., & Beardslee, W. R. (2012). The effects of poverty on the mental, emotional, and behavioral health of children and youth. *American Psychologist, 67*(4), 272-284.

Young-Walker, L., Stormont, M., Beucke, N., & Ell, W., this issue

Zeleke, Hughes, Tiberi, & Drozda, this issue

Behavioral Symptoms of Homeless Children as a Function of Stress Levels and Parental Interaction

Rachel E. Battaglia and Robert A. Reed

Abstract

Research has demonstrated that exposure to stressors such as poverty, parental stress, and residential instability can increase the risk that certain children may develop behavioral disorders (Masten, Miliotis, Graham-Bermann, Ramirez, & Neemann, 1993). The homeless population is exposed to numerous stressors en route to, and during homelessness. The population of families who are homeless continues to rise steadily. In fact, it is the fastest growing population within the population of homeless individuals. Understanding the relationships between certain stressors and behaviors will ultimately help us to effectively identify and assist these families. This research explored the relation between parental stress, parent-child dysfunctional interactions, child stress and, internalizing and externalizing behaviors in children in a homeless population. Participants were parents and their children aged 1-18 years who were homeless. A pattern emerged from the data revealing a positive correlation between parental stress and externalizing and internalizing behaviors among children. Also, as reports of parental stress levels increased, they also reported an increase in dysfunctional parent-child interactions.

Key Words: homelessness, homeless children, homeless families, parental stress

Homeless families are the most rapidly increasing population among the homeless in the United States (Cumella, Grattan, & Vostanis, 1997). Families account for one third of the homeless population; approximately 1.5 million children are homeless every year (Kilmer, Cook, Custro, Strater, & Haber, 2012). Over 20% of children in America are living in a household with incomes below the federal poverty line and are potentially at risk of losing stable housing (Yoshikawa, Aber, & Beardslee, 2012). In the 1980s, the availability of low cost, affordable housing decreased; yet minimum wage did not increase (Rosenberg, Solarz, & Bailey, 1991). This trend continues today; in fact, the United States recently experienced a housing crisis with an increase in poverty levels (Nabors, Proescher, & DeSilva, 2001). Many heads of households have been left without an income; many families' homes have been foreclosed (Kilmer et al., 2012). The prevalence of homelessness in any individual's lifetime in the United States may be the highest among all developed countries (Haber & Toro, 2004). The most common precipitating factor for homelessness is simply extreme poverty (Rosenberg et al., 1991).

Research most often focuses on the lives of single adult homeless individuals (Cumella et al., 1997; Haber & Toro, 2004) instead of studying homeless families and children. Homeless children are exposed to numerous risk factors such as loss of friends, school disruptions, exposure to strangers, loss of familiar surroundings, and threatening situations in shelters and the streets (Douglass, 1996; Kilmer et al., 2012; Wood, Valdez, Hayaski, & Shen, 1990). Exposure to these risk factors increases a homeless child's chances of developing behavioral problems. Adverse Childhood Experiences (ACE) are known to have negative and long-lasting effects on a child's health and their well-being. (Sacks, Murphey, & Moore, 2014). The most common ACE reported in the United States is poverty, with homelessness being an extreme form of poverty.

Behavioral and Emotional Disorders in Homeless Children

Behavioral and emotional disorders have been documented at high rates in the homeless child population (Cumella et al., 1997; Graham-Bermann, Coupet, Egler, & Mattis, 1996). Homeless children frequently do poorly on measures of language development, fine and gross motor development, and personal-social development (Wood et al., 1990) in addition to showing higher rates of other developmental delays (Cumella et al., 1997; Zima, Wells, & Freeman, 1994). Zima et al. (1994) found that children experiencing homelessness were one and a half times more likely than children in the general population to have symptoms of a behavioral disorder. In the United Kingdom, researchers have documented eating problems, sleep disturbances, over-activity, and aggression in homeless children (Cumella et al., 1997). Zima et al. found that homeless children were 20 times more likely than the general population of children to exhibit depressive symptoms.

Stress Before Behavioral Disorders in Homeless Children

Traditional risk factors for children's stress related disorders are poverty and living in a single parent household; however, homeless children are exposed to a unique set of stressful circumstances. These circumstances include frequent moving and discontinuity of school at a young age (Zima et al., 1994). Masten et al. (1993) found that homeless children were exposed to twice as many stressors as children who are economically disadvantaged but not homeless. Violence and aggression are associated with social isolation and relation problems among homeless children (Anooshian, 2005). Instability can deteriorate physical, mental, and emotional development in children (Kilmer et al. 2012; Rosenberg et al., 1991).

Relationship with Parents

Cumella et al. (1997) found the most frequently cited reason for homelessness, besides poverty, was escape from violence. Another study found that 88% of homeless parents reported being a victim of violence (Anooshian, 2005). It is not uncommon for homeless children to experience severe physical abuse by a parent; it has been estimated that homeless children are severely physically abused at rates around 72%. Specifically, Kennedy (2007) found: 48% of homeless children were slapped by a parent; 22% were beaten by a caregiver; and 5% reported that a parent or caregiver used a knife or gun on them. These statistics are not only startling, but are important because harsh, punitive parenting has been shown to increase externalizing behaviors in children (Leve, Kim, & Pears, 2005). Physical violence is not the only cause for increased stress in homeless children. Parents unsupportive towards their child increase psychological and emotional distress in that child (White & Renk, 2011). Harpaz-Rotem, Rosenheck, and Desai (2009) found that emotional and behavioral problems in children fluctuated with changes in maternal PTSD symptoms.

Violence and familial dysfunction contribute to children's development of mental health problems and can lead to depression, substance abuse, and running away (Ferguson, 2009). Homeless parents are less likely to be aware of symptoms of depression or behavioral problems in their children (Zima et al., 1994). Haber and Toro (2004) found that homeless mothers provide less warmth and stimulation to infants because their psychological resources are spent coping with the loss of a home. Parents, both mothers and fathers, who identify as having high stress levels are more likely to have children with behavior problems. When parents feel they have been deprived of material possessions, they experience stress and are more likely to be unresponsive or harsh towards their children (Yoshikawa et al., 2012).

There is a strong correlation between homelessness and interference with effective parenting and the challenges of establishing a parent-child bond. Coercive interactions increase child distress (Leve et al., 2005). Unhealthy relations between parent and child are exacerbated in the homeless environment and are significant predictors of emotional distress and eventually externalizing behaviors (Masten et al., 1993). These parents are less likely to have stable supportive social relations to act as a protective factor (Cumella et al., 1997). Maternal mental health and education level could serve as protective factor for children, even when they are faced with extreme poverty or economical dysfunction, yet homeless mothers most often have low levels of education.

Externalizing Behaviors

The inability for a child to control behavior in an emotional situation can lead to inappropriate behavior and aggression (Anooshian, 2005). Masten et al. (1993) found that homeless and economically disadvantaged children display significantly higher rates of externalizing behaviors than normative samples of same aged children. Specifically, they had higher rates of hitting adults and other children as well as frequent temper tantrums and delinquency (Wood et al., 1990). There is an association between violence witnessed by homeless children and aggressive behaviors. It makes sense that homeless children who experience more violence would display more aggression. Homeless children scored significantly higher than normative samples on specific measure of aggression, delinquency, and social problems syndromes (Masten et al., 1993).

Co-Occuring Internalizing Behaviors

Traditionally, internalizing behaviors and externalizing behaviors are measured separately and are considered to be two different diagnostic classes (Fanti & Henrich, 2010). However, it is important to evaluate internalizing disorders along with externalizing disorders because they often co-occur. In fact, the risk factors are similar for both types of disorders including: low socioeconomic status, maternal depression, difficult temperament, low levels of social support, daily life interferences, and negative home environment (Fanti & Henrich, 2010). Living without stable housing is the defining characteristic of homeless families and places the entire family at risk for more traumatic experiences. Understanding the relation between these experiences and the above mentioned factors will be important in creating informed interventions for the homeless family population (Kilmer et al., 2012).

The Risk Amplification Model (RAM) draws from other theories that explore the impact of parenting and the family environment on development of social isolation, anti-social behavior, and delinquency (Haber & Toro, 2004). According to this theory, the factor of having a nurturing parent is most influential when a child is young. Research suggests that many homeless parents produce lower quality parenting. This lower quality parenting coupled with exposure to deviance and antisocial adults reduce the effects of nurturing parenting. Homelessness must be seen as an amplifier for social marginalization, conduct disorders, and antisocial behavior (Haber & Toro, 2004). Externalizing behaviors are seriously disruptive. Childhood aggression remains a strong predictor of violence and crime in adults (Liu, 2004). Five to seven percent of children with externalizing behaviors follow the life-course projection of externalizing behaviors (Fanti & Henrich, 2010). Co-occurrence of internalizing and externalizing behaviors decreases the opportunity for children to develop necessary social skills and increases the likelihood that the child will experience further isolation. These children with co-occurrence are found to be more disruptive and depressed overall (El-Sheikh, Hinnant, Kelly, & Erath, 2010). The cycle continues to follow the RAM. The longer a child suffers from internalizing and externalizing disorders, the harder it is to treat the behavioral disorder.

Significance of research. The purpose of this study was to examine internalizing and externalizing behaviors in homeless children ages 1-18 years and to examine the relation these behaviors have with the stress levels of the children, the parents, and the parent-child interactions. Previous research has examined the developmental and physical delays experienced by children in the homeless population as well as the rate of childhood illnesses in the homeless population. Other research has focused on the lives of adult homeless individuals and "street children," mostly over the age of 18 years, who are not living with their families.

Limitations in current research include studies where only the mother is accessible, rather than having access to the children and the mothers. Moreover, parental stress is not routinely assessed to determine whether parental stress is related to the parents' perceptions of behaviors and acting out in children (Wood et al., 1990); specifically, how a dysfunctional parental relationship with the child affects behavioral problems. Other limitations and inconsistencies have been found in research with homeless children (Douglass, 1996). Research on homeless children was conducted most often 10 or more years ago, though it is well-documented that homelessness continues to be a problem in the United States. The variables have been identified as parental stress (PS), parent-child dysfunctional interactions (PCI), child stress (CS), internalizing behaviors (INT) in the child, and externalizing behaviors (EXT) in the child. It is predicted that there will be strong positive relations between each of these variables.

Specifically, there will be a significant positive relation between child stress levels and internalizing behaviors within the homeless population, a significant positive relation between child stress levels and externalizing behaviors in children within the homeless population, a significant positive relation between parent-child relational dysfunction and parental stress within the homeless population, a significant positive relation between parent-child relational dysfunction and child stress within the homeless population, a significant positive relation between parent-child relational dysfunction and externalizing behaviors in children within the homeless population, a significant positive relation between parent-child relational dysfunction and internalizing behaviors in children within the homeless population, a significant positive relation between parental stress and internalizing behaviors in children within the homeless population, and a significant positive relation between parental stress and externalizing behaviors in children within the homeless population.

Methods

Research participants were homeless adults and their children (37 male children, 28 female children) ranging in age from 1- 18 years (M = 8.5; SD = 4.99). The mean number of months that participants reported being homeless was 18.6 months (SD = 24.53). See Table 1 for additional demographic information. Demographic information for the parental age, gender, or race/ethnicity was purposely not collected; many other research studies used this information to make guesses about reasons for homelessness. For the purpose of this study, reasons for homelessness were not relevant because it is assumed that underlying poverty was the cause of homelessness.

Parents completed a demographic questionnaire and two rating scales: one about their child's behaviors and the other regarding their parental stress levels and perceptions of their relationship with their child. Children ages 6-18 years completed a stress rating scale, while parents assisted children under the age of six years with filling out the stress rating scale or filled it out according to the child's experiences. As is typical in previously studied homeless families, the head of the household was most often a single female.

Measures

The following measures were used: (a) a demographic questionnaire; (b) The Social Readjustment Rating Scale (Holmes & Rahe, 1967); (c) The Parental Stress Index-Short Form (Abidin, 1990); and (d) The Child Behavior Checklist (Achenbach & Rescorla, 2001).

Demographic questionnaire. A questionnaire developed by the investigator was used to gather basic demographic information such as age, gender, race, occupational status, educational attainment, marital status, number of children in family less than 18 years old, number of moves in the last year, and number of months homeless.

Table 1:
Family Demographic Information

Variable	N	%	Mean	Std. dev.
Age of child (years)	65	-	8.5 (1.5- 18 years)	4.99
Months homeless	65	-	18.6	24.53
Gender (male)	37			
(female)	28			
Parent relationship status				
Married	2	3%		
Single	37	56.9%		
Separated	11	16.9%		
Committed relation	8	12.3%		
Divorced	7	10.8%		
Education of parent				
Some high school	17	26.2%		
High school grad	14	21.5%		
Some college	23	35.4%		
College grad	10	15.4%		
Master's	1	1.5%		
Employment of parent				
Full-Time	14	21.5%		
Part-Time	13	20%		
Unemployed	38	58.5%		
Living situation				
Friends/rel.	13	20%		
Homeless shelter	73	56.9%		
Domestic shelter	9	13.8%		
Facing eviction	6	9.2%		

Child Behavior Checklist (CBCL; Achenbauch & Rescorla, 2001). This checklist includes 118 symptoms that are rated by a parent or caregiver about their child on a 3-point scale. The CBCL provides T scores for three global dimensions: Total Problems, Internalizing, and Externalizing. Reliability as measured by Cronbach's alpha was found to be .92 for Internalizing and Externalizing Behaviors Scales (Achenbach et al., 2008). The Externalizing behavior scale has a correlation of .62 with the DSM-IV checklist for conduct disorder and a correlation of .88 on the BASC Externalizing scale (Achenbach & Rescorla, 2001). The Internalizing behavior scale has a correlation of .59 with the DSM-IV checklist for depression and a correlation of .83 on the BASC Internalizing scale (Achenbach & Rescorla, 2001). Cronbach's Alpha for this study was .67. The parent filled out this form.

Parental Stress Index Short Form (PSI-SF, Abidin, 1995). The PSI-SF is a 36 item instrument that measures parental distress, parent-child dysfunctional interactions, and difficult child using a 6 point Likert scale. Internal reliability as measured by Cronbach's alpha was found to be between .80 and .91 for the different scales (Hill & Rose, 2009). The Total Stress scale reliability was .91, the validity .94 (Abidin, 1995). The parent filled out this form. Cronbach's Alpha for this study was .73.

The Social Readjustment Rating Scale (SRRS; Holmes & Rahe, 1967). The SRRS includes 43 isolated and ongoing experiences and life events that vary in appeal and ability of the child or adult to influence desirability (Rafferty & Shinn, 1991). The respondent checks a box next to the item if they have experienced it. The items measure the intensity of recent life events and then provide a numerical score to estimate the individual's stress level (Holmes & Rahe, 1967). The SRRS is the most widely used measurement of individual experience of stress for adults and children (McGrath & Burkhart, 2005). All coefficients of correlation were found to be above 0.90, and for those under age 30 years it is .96; Kendall's coefficient of concordance (W) was .48, significant at $p = < 0.0005$ (Holmes & Rahe, 1967). The child filled out this form with assistance from an adult if needed.

Procedure

Participants were mostly recruited through local county agencies that serve homeless families. Service coordinators were provided with packets (with self-addressed, pre-paid return labels) to hand out to interested families. Some families heard of the research through word-of-mouth and contacted their service coordinators to request to participate. Some participants were recruited through soup kitchens and/or organizations that serve single mothers. Participants were considered homeless if they were living in a homeless shelter, domestic shelter, living with friends, living with family, or were living in a home while facing eviction/foreclosure. The participants were recruited from two different cities; one mid-sized mid-Atlantic city and one large mid-West city.

Parents completed a demographic questionnaire and two rating scales; one about their child's behaviors and the other regarding their parental stress levels and perceptions of their relationship with their child. Children ages 6-18 years completed a stress rating scale, while parents assisted children under the age of 6 years with filling out the stress rating scale or filled it out according to the child's experiences. A total of 100 packets were distributed, mostly through the mail with return postage provided. A total of 69 packets were returned; however, four packets were incomplete and subsequently discarded. Forms were specific to over the age of 6 years or under the age of 6 years.

Results

All measures were hand-scored and entered into an SPSS database and cross-checked for errors. The variables were identified as parental stress (PS), parent-child dysfunctional interactions (PCI), child stress (CS), internalizing behaviors (INT) in the child, and externalizing behaviors (EXT) in the child.

To test each hypothesis, several comparisons of the data were conducted. Each hypothesis included two non-parametric variables with one level; therefore, the Spearman Correlation was used for each comparison. According to guidelines for using Spearman Correlations, it is estimated that the sample size should be approximately 109 (N > 104 + k, k = 5) or greater pairs of participants (caregiver and child) (Warner, 2008). The actual sample size was 65 pairs of participants (caregiver and child).

Data collection began on October 30, 2013, and continued until March 30, 2014, to fit with dissertation timelines. One hundred packets were distributed, 69 were returned with 65 completed packages. Number of months homeless ranged from one month to 156 months, indicating a positively skewed sample. It was expected that this sample would be somewhat positively skewed. Histogram and box plots indicated that scores on the variables Parental Stress (PS), Parent-Child Dysfunctional Interaction (PCI), and Child Stress (CS) were not normally distributed, while scores on the variables Internalizing (INT) behaviors in children and Externalizing (EXT) behaviors in children were normally distributed. See Table 2 for statistical information on each variable.

Table 2:
Variable Characteristics

Variable	Mean	Std. dev.
PS	30.49	8.84
PCI	23.87	9.84
CS	198.78	125.81
INT	50.96	13.09
EXT	51.70	12.18

Table 3 highlights the results of the Spearman Correlations. The relation between PS and PCI was statistically significant ($r = .53$, $p = .01$). The relation between PS and INT was statistically significant ($r = .31$, $p = .05$). The relation between PS and EXT was statistically significant ($r = .33$, $p = .01$). The relation between PCI and CS was not statistically significant ($r = .02$, $p = .02$). The relation between PCI and INT was statistically significant ($r = .34$, $p = .01$). The relation between PCI and EXT was statistically significant ($r = .61$, $p = .01$). The relation between CS and INT was not statistically significant ($r = .20$, $p = .19$). The relation between CS and EXT was statistically significant ($r = .10$, $p = .09$). An additional Spearman correlation was conducted to assess if the number of months homeless was related to any of the variables (PS, PCI, CS, INT, EXT). The results indicated that the number of months homeless was not related to any of the variables; meaning the level of stress was not increased or decreased as the number of months increased or decreased. Coefficient of Determination was conducted to assess how much of INT was affecting EXT and vice versa. The results, $r^2 = .26$ for INT and EXT, indicating that approximately 25% of internalizing behaviors could be accounted for by externalizing behaviors and 25% of externalizing behaviors could be accounted for by internalizing behaviors.

Table 3:
Spearman Correlations

Variable	Spearman's rho	Significance level (p)
PS r PCI	.526	0.01, two tailed
PS r INT	.310	0.05, two tailed
PS r EXT	.332	0.01, two tailed
PCI r CS	.020	0.02
PCI r INT	.337	0.01, two tailed
PCI r EXT	.606	0.01, two tailed
CS r INT	.196	0.19
CS r EXT	.097	0.09
Months r PS	-.102	-0.10
Months r PCI	.016	0.02
Months r CS	-.032	-0.03
Months r INT	.008	0.00
Months r EXT	-.118	-0.12

Discussion

Homelessness is not a new problem in our society; neither are behavior disorders among children. It was difficult to find journal articles exploring the relationship between homelessness and behavior disorders in children. The first prediction, that there would be a significant positive relation between child stress levels and internalizing behaviors in the child was not found. The second prediction, that there would be a significant positive relation between child stress levels and externalizing behaviors in the child was also not found. There are several potential explanations, which are explored in the limitations section. The average age of the child in this study was approximately eight and a half years, with the most common reported age of the child being 2 years old. Children less than 6 years of age did not complete the forms themselves; therefore, the measure of their stress levels are based on parent perceptions.

The next prediction, that there would be a significant positive relation between parent-child relational dysfunction and parental stress, was significant. The parent filled out both forms that measured parental stress and parent-child relational dysfunction. It makes sense that these perspectives were aligned. As reported (Yoshikawa et al., 2012) when parents experience more stress in their own life, they are likely to increase dysfunctional interactions between themselves and their children. Many homeless parents are socially isolated themselves and are lacking stable, supportive relationships with other adults (Cumella et al., 1997). Without supports to turn to for stress relief, homeless parents are left to cope with their stress on their own. The fourth prediction, that there would be a significant positive relationship between parent-child relational dysfunction and child stress was not found. One potential explanation is that this may be attributed to the most common age of the participants being two years old, so the report of stress was largely based on parent perception; on the other hand, previous studies have found that dysfunctional interactions between the parent and the child, especially those that are verbally charged, may not immediately register with the child (Ferguson, 2009). That is, the child may not immediately recognize the interaction as distressing or dysfunctional, rather their stress levels increase over time and the child simply feels distressed without understanding the reasons for their distress (Ferguson, 2009).

The fifth prediction, that there would be a significant positive relation between parent-child relational dysfunction and externalizing behaviors in the child was significant. The sixth prediction, that there would be a significant positive relation between parent-child relational dysfunction and internalizing behaviors in the child was also significant. These findings add support for the notion that children may not recognize dysfunctional interactions with their parent as stressful, rather they can feel distressed without knowing exactly why. It is important to note that the measures used in the study provide a number for total stressors, but it does not ask respondents to draw conclusions about what is causing the stress. Also, there are no test items asking about dysfunctional parental interactions or parental stress in general. These results are consistent with the literature showing the more stressed a child feels, the more dysfunctional behaviors will be displayed (Ferguson, 2009). Familial dysfunction has been found to be related to the development of mental health disorders in children (Ferguson, 2009). Many of the children in this study were young, and dysfunctional parent-child interactions at a young age can create a disorganized attachment between the parent and the child (Yoshikawa et al., 2012). Having a disorganized attachment with the child would certainly increase dysfunctional parent-child interactions. In fact, when a child feels unsupported by the parent, psychological distress is likely (White & Renk, 2011). The current study did not measure attachment types or styles; however, this would be an interesting direction for research.

The seventh prediction, that there would be a significant positive relation between parental stress and internalizing behaviors in the child was significant as well as the eighth prediction, that there would be a significant positive relation between parental stress and externalizing behaviors in the child. Parental stress makes it difficult for parents to be emotionally supportive towards their children (Graham-Bermann et al., 1996). Homeless mothers report high levels of stress and this personal stress may be preventing the mother from recognizing the impact of those stressors on her child's emotional well-being. The RAM model uses stressors to predict the increase of behavior disorders in the child, with those families with high stress levels also having children with high levels of behavior disorders (Haber & Toro, 2004). This pattern emerged in this study as well. The more stressed the parent, the higher the number of negative behaviors the parent endorsed in the child; externalizing and internalizing. The young age of the children in this study coupled with this pattern of increasing behaviors according to increasing parental stress is concerning.

Of the statistically significant relationships, the strongest was between the increase in parental stress and the degree to which the parent experienced the interactions with the child as dysfunctional. Likely, these two variables are related because the parent reports his/her own perceptions for each of these variables. Results indicate that the more stress the parent felt related to parenting, the more likely the parent indicates the relationship with the child is problematic. However, it is important to note that items on this scale also include questions about lack of social support, disagreement with the child's other parent, and a poor bond between the parent and the child. As such, a high score here could be derived from several sources. All of these factors have been shown to be present within the homeless population. Buckner, Bassuk, Weinreb, & Brooks (1999) found that the strongest predictor of behavioral problems in children was the maternal distress. Another study also found that conflict between the parent and the child was related to maternal distress (Graham-Bermann et al., 1996). It follows that maternal distress is related to dysfunction in the parent-child relation and a subsequent increase in externalizing behaviors on behalf of the child.

This creates a cycle where parent and child are trapped and continue to increase dysfunction. When a parent feels a lesser bond towards their children, they are more likely to engage in punitive parenting practices such as physical abuse (Kilmer et al., 2012). Physical abuse towards children has been shown to increase externalizing behaviors in children (Leve et al., 2005). When a child is exhibiting externalizing behaviors, the child should also be assessed to rule out physical abuse.

Limitations of the Study

This study utilized a sample of convenience, and as such, one cannot be assured that the sample accurately represents the population that one would hope it represents. Another limitation of this study is the small sample size. While a return rate of 65% percent of the instruments distributed is generally good, the sample size was lower (n = 65) than recommended by the power analysis. As such, the smaller sample may not be able to detect meaningful differences. Recruitment of homeless individuals was very difficult, as they are often ostracized by society and remain hidden. For example, those living in cars may not come to the attention of social service agencies. Some participants initially recruited indicated that they did not want to fill out the forms because of the title of the research study included the word "homeless." In addition, those without any type of housing were difficult to contact, mailing forms was not possible, and they were not always reliable with returning forms. A total of 100 hundred families were identified as meeting the criteria for the study and expressed willingness to participate; however, only 69 families returned packets and only 65 were completed entirely and were included in the data set.

Another limitation of this study was the range of months of homelessness experienced by each participant in this study. Homelessness ranged from 1 month to 156 months. Because of the skewed range for this sample, it may have affected how participants responded to the survey instruments. For example, stress levels may wax and wane for individuals throughout the course of their experiences with homelessness. Individuals may experience more stress in the first month of homelessness as they adjust to their new surroundings. Some individuals may experience more stress in the middle of their homeless experience and they may feel that there is no hope. Others may find more stress towards the end of their homelessness when they are attempting to secure services and function without the support of social service agencies.

A large number of participants (N = 37, 56.9%) were living in homeless shelters, while some participants (N = 9, 13.8%) were living in domestic shelters. Together, individuals living in shelters of some type comprised 70% of the participants for this study. Although this study's aim was to collect information on families living in less visible homeless situations, it captured more of the visible homeless families who were involved with homeless agencies already.

The measures selected for this study were partially chosen because of the convenience and price. This study was originally completed to fulfill the requirement for a dissertation; thus the SRRS was selected because it is readily available and free. While other research studies have used the SRRS for children and to measure stress in children, there were other, more expensive measures that may have produced a more accurate reflection of stress in young children. It was not anticipated that so many of children in the study would be under the age of six years.

Implications for Future Research, Program, or Policy

The variable length of homelessness that emerged in this study was notable. Additional research should examine if stress varies during periods of homelessness. It's likely that parental needs change throughout the course of homelessness. It would also be important to compare types of homelessness to stress levels, specifically parental stress levels. For instance, perhaps the parental stress is greater in a homeless shelter as compared to living in one's home while facing eviction or being physically homeless, or perhaps the parental stress level is greater when living with friends or extended family. It would be beneficial to learn more about the interactions in families experiencing different types of homelessness so that the family's specific needs could be addressed through informed interventions.

Given that this study's strongest correlations were between the level of parental distress and the level of dysfunction in the parent-child interactions, and the level of dysfunction of parent-child interactions and externalizing behaviors in children, this suggests that helpful services could target the parents' adjustment to their living situation and overall adjustment (Abidin, 1995). Helping parents to adjust more quickly and more efficiently could potentially allow them the mental freedom to focus more on their parenting and their relationship with their child.

Therapeutic services could also work to improve the parents' sense of competence and self-esteem (Abidin, 1995). The more competent the parents feel, the more likely they are to feel they can manage the interactions with their children. Increasing the positivity in the parent-child relationship would likely reduce the level of dysfunction in that relationship.

Conclusions

Homeless families comprise approximately one third of all homeless individuals living in America and 1 in 50 children experience some type of homelessness each year (Kilmer et al., 2012). Bringing the needs of this population of children to the attention of schools and community agencies should be a high priority for clinicians and policy makers. Identifying appropriate interventions along with measuring parent and child outcomes is required for this underserved population. It is imperative to intervene in an effective way to protect the future of one of the most vulnerable populations in the United States. Strengthening families and increasing parenting skills for homeless parents has the potential to improve the well-being of homeless children and reduce the impact of this public health crisis.

References

Abidin, R.R. (1990). *Parenting Stress Index-manual, revised edition.* Charlottesville, VA: Pediatric Psychology Press.

Abidin, R. R. (1995). *Parenting Stress Index, 3rd edition, professional manual.* Lutz, FL: PAR.

Achenbach, T. M., Becker, A., Döpfner, M., Heiervang, E., Roessner, V., Steinhausen, H., & Rothenberger, A. (2008). Multicultural assessment of child and adolescent psychopathology with ASEBA and SDQ instruments: Research findings, applications, and future directions. *Journal of Child Psychology and Psychiatry, 49,* 251-275. doi:10.1111/j.1469-7610.2007.01867.x

Achenbach, T. M., & Rescorla, L. A. (2001). *Manual for the ASEBA school-age forms & profiles.* Burlington, VT: University of Vermont, Research Center for Children, Youth, & Families.

Anooshian, L. J. (2005). Violence and aggression in the lives of homeless children. *Journal of Family Violence, 20,* 373-387. doi:10.1007/s10896-005-7799-3

Buckner, J. C., Bassuk, E. L., Weinreb, L. F., & Brooks, M. G. (1999). Homelessness and its relation to the mental health and behavior of low-income school-age children. *Developmental Psychology, 35,* 246-257.

Cumella, S., Grattan, E., & Vostanis, P. (1997). The mental health of children in homeless families and their contact with health, education and social services. *Health and Social Care in Community, 6,* 331-342.

Douglass, A. (1996). Rethinking the effects of homelessness on children: Resiliency and competency. *Child Welfare League of America, LXXV,* 742-751. doi: 0009-4021/96/060741-12

El-Sheikh, M., Hinnant, J. B., Kelly, R. J., & Erath, S. (2010). Maternal psychological control and child internalizing symptoms: Vulnerability and protective factors across bioregulatory and ecological domains. *The Journal of Child Psychology and Psychiatry, 51,* 188-198. doi: 10.1111/j.1469-7610.2009.02140.x

Fanti, K. A., & Henrich, C. C. (2010). Trajectories of pure and co-occurring internalizing and externalizing problems from age 2 to age 12: Findings from the national institute of child health and human development study of early child care. *Developmental Psychology, 46,* 1159-1175. doi: 10.1037/a0020659

Ferguson, K. M. (2009). Exploring the psychosocial and behavioral adjustment outcomes of multi-type abuse among homeless young adults. *Social Work Research, 33,* 219-230.

Graham-Bermann, S. A., Coupet, S., Egler, L., & Mattis, J. (1996). Interpersonal relationships and adjustment of children in homeless and economically distressed families. *Journal of Clinical Child Psychology, 25,* 250-261.

Haber, M. G., & Toro, P. A. (2004). Homelessness among families, children, and adolescents: An ecological-developmental perspective. *Clinical Child and Family Psychology Review, 7,* 123-164.

Harpez-Rotem, Ilan, Rosenheck, R.A., & Desai, R. (2009). Assessing the effects of maternal symptoms and homelessness on the mental health problems in their children. *Child and Adolescent Mental Health, 14,* 168-174. doi: 10.1111/j.1475-3588.2008.00519.x

Hill, C., & Rose J. (2009). Parenting stress in mothers of adults with and intellectual disability: Parental cognitions in relation to child characteristics and family support. *Journal of Intellectual Disability Research, 53,* 969-980. doi: 10.1111/j.1356-2788.2009.01207.x

Holmes, T. H., & Rahe, R. H. (1967). The social readjustment rating scale. *Journal of Psychosomatic Research, 11,* 213-218.

Kennedy, A. C. (2007). Homelessness, violence exposure, and school participation among urban adolescent mothers. *Journal of Community Psychology, 35,* 639-654. doi:10.1002/jcop.20169

Kilmer, R.P, Cook, J. R., Crusto, C., Strater K. P., & Haber, M. G. (2012). Understanding the ecology and development of children and families experiencing homelessness: Implications for practice, supportive services, and policy. *American Journal of Orthopsychiatry, 82,* 389-401. doi: 10.1111/j.1939-0025.2012.01160.x

Leve, L. D., Kim, H. K., & Pears, K. C. (2005). Childhood temperament and family environment as predictors of internalizing and externalizing trajectories from ages 5 to 17. *Journal of Abnormal Child Psychology, 33,* 505-520. doi:10.1007/s10802-005-6734-7

Liu, J. (2004). Childhood externalizing behavior: Theory and implications. *Journal of Child and Adolescent Psychiatric Nursing, 17,* 93-103.

Masten, A. S., Miliotis, D., Graham-Bermann, S. A., Ramirez, M., & Neemann, J. (1993). Children in homeless families: Risks to mental health and development. *Journal of Consulting and Clinical Psychology, 61,* 335-343.

McGrath, R.E.V. & Burkhart, B.R. (2005). Measuring life stress: a comparison of the predictive validity of different scoring systems for the social readjustment rating scale.

Menke, E.M. (2000). Comparison of the stressors and coping behaviors of homeless, previously homeless, and never homeless poor children. *Issues in Mental Health Nursing, 21*, 691-710.

Nabors, L., Proescher, E., & DeSilva, M. (2001). School-based mental health prevention activities for homeless and at-risk youth. *Child & Youth Care Forum, 30*, 3-18.

Rafferty, Y., & Shinn, M. (1991). The impact of homelessness on children. *American Psychologist, 46*, 1170-1179.

Rosenberg, A. A., Solarz, A. L., & Bailey, W. A. (1991). Psychology and homelessness: A public policy and advocacy agenda. *American Psychologist, 46*, 1239-1244.

Sacks, V., Murphey D., & Moore, K. (2014). Adverse Childhood Experience: National and state-level prevalence. *Research Brief Child Trends, 2014-28*.

Warner, R. M. (2008). *Applied Statistics: From bivariate through multivariate techniques.* Thousand Oaks, CA: Sage Publications, Inc.

White, R., & Renk, K. (2011). Externalizing behavior problems during adolescence: An ecological perspective. *Journal of Child and Family Studies, 21*, 158-171. doi: 10.1007/s10826-011-9459-y

Wood, D. L., Valdez, R. B., Hayaski, T., & Shen, A. (1990). Health of homeless children and housed, poor children. *Pediatrics, 86*, 858-866.

Yoshikawa, H., Aber, J. L., & Beardslee, W. R. (2012). The effects of poverty on the mental, emotional, and behavioral health of children and youth: Implications for prevention. *American Psychologist, 67*, 272-284. doi:10.1037/a0028015

Zima, B. T., Wells, K. B., & Freeman, H. E. (1994). Emotional and behavioral problems and severe academic delays among sheltered homeless children in Los Angeles county. *American Journal of Public Health, 84*, 260-264.

Healthcare and Educational Services Used by Children with Autism Spectrum Disorders in Poverty

Waganesh A. Zeleke, Tammy L. Hughes, Amy E. Tiberi, and Natalie A. Drozda

Abstract

This study examined children with autism spectrum disorder (ASD) who live below the Federal Poverty Line (FPL) using data from the 2011 *Survey of Pathway to Diagnosis and Services* national data set (n = 1725). When compared to children with ASD in homes above the FPL, results indicate these children are similar in age at the time of diagnosis and symptom severity, and treatment needs and insurance status are comparable. However, how parents approached seeking a diagnosis and their ability to obtain intervention services varied by poverty status. Parents of children with ASD living below the FPL found school providers were more responsive to their concerns whereas parents above the FPL found their health care providers were more responsive. Recommended outreach efforts are suggested and described.

Key Words: poverty, autism, early intervention, access to healthcare, educational services

The negative effects of poverty on individuals and society are widely documented. For example, the association between poverty and poor physical health (KewalRamani, 2007), poor school performance and educational attainment (Sirin, 2005), and emotional and behavioral disorders (Fujiura & Yamaki, 2000) are found throughout the literature. Children born into impoverished families are at greater risks for developmental delays and disorders (Fujiura & Yamaki, 2000); also, children in chronic poverty conditions before the age of five show the least resilience to the effects of poverty (Bradley & Corwyn, 2002).

One of the major barriers for families living in poverty is access to early diagnostic and intervention services. Studies have consistently supported the conclusions of Schulzinger, Haifley, and Allen (2003) that "poor children and children of color have worse access to health care and as a result often start life several steps behind their wealthier and healthier white peers" (6). Parents often lack adequate knowledge about when and where to access services; they may access health services only when a problem has reached a crisis level rather than seeking on-going preventive care. Additionally, stress and cultural expectations can interfere with health care seeking (Liptak et al., 2008), all of which can prevent children from gaining crucial medical care during their formative years (Longtin & Principe, 2014).

For children with autism spectrum disorder (ASD), early identification and intervention services are considered critical for the most effective outcomes (e.g., reducing symptoms, improvements in language, and cognitive ability; Hume, Bellini, & Pratt, 2005; National Research Council, 2001). As such, children with ASD living in poverty may be at particular risk for not receiving important and timely service options.

Poverty and Access to Services

The federal government uses several measures to determine poverty levels (e.g., poverty thresholds and poverty guidelines; United States Department of Health and Human Services, 2015). The Federal Poverty Level (FPL) is a common term that references the poverty guidelines definition; these guidelines are issued by the Department of Health and Human Services and are important because they are used to determine financial eligibility for several government-subsidized programs (*42 U.S.C. 9902 (2)*). As of 2016, there were 15 million, or 21%, of American children below the FPL (Supplemental Poverty Measure, 2016). Even with guidance on how to define poverty, FPL is still a very broad term and may not be used in academic research. Instead, Supplemental Poverty Measures (2016) and other terms (e.g., socioeconomic status [SES] or socioeconomic deficits [SED] among others) may be used among research teams. Although definitional concerns can impair statistical comparisons across studies, there is a general consensus that poverty is a risk factor alone and can amplify other risks present for individuals (National Institute for Health Care Management [NIHCM], 2008; Owens & Shaw, 2003).

Poverty and Health Care

Despite federal initiatives (e.g., Medicaid and several funded programs through the Patient Protection and Affordable Care Act, which is commonly referred to as the Affordable Care Act, [ACA], U.S.C. § 18001, 2010) that have increased the availability of health care services to a large majority of American citizens, there continues to be a lack of health resources for specific groups of people (i.e., individuals of color and those living below the FPL). When these data are viewed from different vantage points, researchers found: a) the prevalence of disease and disabilities remains higher for those who are impoverished than for those who are not, b) individuals of color are overrepresented among impoverished groups, which is strongly associated with poor health (NIHCM, 2008) and c) individuals living in poverty that are of minority status and living in non-urban areas report lower use of health care services (Thomas, Ellis, McLaurin, Daniels, & Morrissey, 2007). The greatest amount of poverty in the United States is found in single-family households, which impedes proper care (Birenbaum, 2002) and risk factors for disabilities (Fujiura & Yamaki, 2000).

Children, in particular, are affected by health care disparities. Children of color are more likely to be uninsured than their white counterparts, which has been shown to adversely affect health, and thus, growth and development through adulthood (Schulzinger et al., 2003). Indeed, Latino and black children are four times as likely as whites to self-report being in fair or poor health (Longtin & Principe, 2014). Lack of insurance is in part due to low levels of parental knowledge regarding the ability to access services through federal programming, especially when parents are undereducated or unemployed. Whereas 95% of children have access to health coverage – the government subsidized insurance, Children's Health Insurance Program (CHIP), is available to any parent regardless of income level – there are still 9 million children who go uninsured (Children's Defense Fund, 2017).

Poverty and Education Services

Given that school failure and emotional and behavioral challenges often accompany children in poverty, how these children access and use school support services, including special education services, needs to be considered (Ferguson, Bovaird, & Muller, 2007; Jensen, 2009). For example, Longtin and Principe (2014) report that poverty conditions are more common among children with disabilities than among children without disabilities. It is estimated that 28% of U.S. children with disabilities are living in poverty (Fujijura & Yamaki, 2000).

The Individuals with Disabilities Education Improvement Act (IDEIA, 2004) is a federal law that requires school districts to *find* all children with disabilities living in their district. *Child Find* (20 U.S.C. 1412 a (3) is the requirement for schools to identify and evaluate all children, birth to 21 years of age, with known or suspected disabilities living in their district catchment area, regardless of where the student attends school (e.g., private, homeschool), and provide them Free and Appropriate Public Education (FAPE). Although IDEIA has been in effect since 1974, districts are still inconsistent in their implementation of services in providing FAPE for students with disabilities. In particular, districts that serve low-SES communities with diverse populations are more likely to have an abundance of referrals for special education, yet the services these students receive may not be individually matched to their disability needs

(Skiba, Poloni-Staudinger, Simmons, Feggins-Azziz, & Chung, 2005). Skiba et. al., have noted an overrepresentation of minority and impoverished students in special education; "factors associated with living in poverty leave children less developmentally ready for schooling and ultimately yield negative academic and behavioral outcomes" (2005, p. 131).

Poverty and Autism

It is estimated that 1 in 68 children will be diagnosed with an ASD (Center for Disease Control [CDC], 2016). The CDC also reports that the total cost per year for children with ASD in the United States is estimated to be between $11.5 billion and $60.9 billion. This economic burden is comprised of medical care, special education services, and lost parental productivity. For Medicaid-enrolled children who are diagnosed with ASD, the cost of care per year is estimated to be $10,709, which is approximately six times more than the average costs of care for children without ASDs (Peacock, Amendah, Ouyang, & Grosse, 2012). Beyond that, costs can vary greatly depending on co-occurring neurodevelopmental disorders, or intellectual disabilities (ID). For impoverished families living under the FPL, the financial burden and stress that accompanies an ASD diagnosis can be unmanageable. For these families in particular, it is essential that they are aware of how to gain access to proper diagnostic services, medical care, and educational support so that the children are not excluded from receiving services during the developmental window that offers the best outcomes for children with ASD.

Service Needs for Children with Autism

Children with ASDs tend to be higher users of health care services due to the complex and pervasive nature of the condition. For example, compared to other children, those with ASD have significantly more total outpatient services and physician visits, and are also prescribed more medications (Bitterman, Daley, Misra,

Carlson, & Markowitz, 2008). Consistent with the research reported above, researchers show that access and use of ASD services are related to parent economic status. Specifically, earlier identification of children with ASD is related to maternal education, race, and ethnicity (Longtin & Principe, 2014) presumably because greater parent education and wealth provide families with resources (Liptak et al., 2008) that poor families do not have access to, and maybe unaware of, or are otherwise distracted with day to day survival (Enwefa, Enwefa, & Jennings, 2006). Relatedly, even when children are receiving services, impoverished parents may be unaware of the services the child is receiving. In 2014, Longtin and Principe found that urban parents who were above the FPL were more aware of health and educational services that their children with ASD received than those below FPL. Parents who are unaware of their child's needs are less likely to serve an active role in their child's care, further disadvantaging poor children (Liptak et al., 2008).

Age of Diagnosis

Although the age of diagnosis for ASD is declining overall, suggesting an increased awareness in parents and healthcare providers, early diagnosis is not equally accessible. According to Mandell, Novak, and Zubritsky (2005), the average age children with ASD are diagnosed is 3.1 years. However, children living below poverty receive diagnoses 0.9 years later than those with incomes above the FPL. The same study suggests that for children living in poverty who do not have a consistent primary care physician, their age of diagnosis averages about 0.5 years later than those children who do have a consistent primary care provider.

One explanation for the discrepancies reported above is that children receiving government-enrolled health care have a longer wait to receive the diagnosis. In a two-year window, 28,722 children were newly diagnosed with ASD just within the Medicaid rolls. The average age of diagnosis for these children was, 64.9 months, or almost 5.5 years old (Mandell, et al., 2010). "Findings show that diagnosis of ASD occurs much later than it should among Medicaid enrolled children" (Mandell, et al., 2010, p. 822). Results also showed that children in large urban and rural counties are diagnosed later, on average, then those in small urban and suburban counties. Additionally, states that employ the CHIP program had variance among the age of diagnosis for youth with ASD. In those states that used a more stringent qualification criterion for CHIP, children are diagnosed at an earlier age.

Some of the barriers to early diagnosis for children with ASDs are similar to those noted in impoverished families including the lack of parental knowledge and support. Data have shown that children who are diagnosed at an earlier age often have parents who are alert to warning signs and symptoms for ASD, and have their children in scheduled well-care appointments (Birenbaum, 2002). For families living in poverty and struggling to make ends meet, gaining proper healthcare and diagnostic services may not be a primary concern. Rather, basic living needs, such as access to transportation, housing, and food take precedent, and in turn their child's developmental trajectory can suffer.

Early Intervention Services

There is general consensus that early intervention services are recommended for all children with an ASD (National Research Council, 2001). This is because children with ASD who receive services prior to age five are reported to make gains more quickly than those with other neurodevelopmental disabilities (Rogers, 1996) and have better outcomes (Liptak et al., 2008; Longtin & Principe, 2014). There is also wide agreement that intervention services need to be tailored to the individual (Li-Grining & Durlik, 2014; Skiba et al., 2005), comprehensively addressing all of the child's needs (Hume et al., 2005), include contact with typical peers (Bitterman et al., 2008) and parental commitment and participation (Hume et al., 2005; Li-Grining & Durlik, 2014). Comprehensive service delivery may include any of the following combination of services:

behavioral supports, classroom supports, consultation, counseling, medical treatment, physical therapy, occupational therapy, speech therapy, social supports, summer services (i.e., year-round school or another educational placement), and parent training and support in order to address deficits in the academic, social, and behavioral domains (Hume et al., 2005).

Healthcare and ASD

For families of children on the autism spectrum, the ACA expanded affordable insurance options, including an expansion within Medicaid. Moreover, the law meant that families could not be turned away from coverage due to their child's diagnosis of ASD, and many families could qualify for additional financial assistance to help pay for premiums and out-of-pocket expenses associated with autism-related care. Another major change that came with ACA was the inclusion of autism screenings for children at 18 months and 24 months (2010). This is included in all health plans, which are covered in the privatized sector, and must be provided without charging copayment or coinsurance (United States Department of Health and Human Services, 2015).

Children are eligible for Medicaid when their families' income is less than the FPL. However, many states have expanded Medicaid eligibility "to include children of families with income as high as 300% of the poverty level" (Mandell et. al., 2010, p. 3). Medicaid covers a high percentage of children who are diagnosed with ASD, and often, these are children with more severe impairments and negative life course trajectories. Some children will qualify for a supplemental secondary insurance through Medicaid as determined by the severity of the impact of their diagnosis rather than poverty status (Semansky, Xie, & Mandell, 2011). Children with ASD are also eligible to be covered under the CHIP program described previously.

Economically distressed families that have children with developmental disabilities are much more likely to realize the barriers to gaining proper treatment than those families that have children who are not developmentally disabled (McGrath, Laflamme, Schwartz, Stransky, & Moeschler, 2009). Insurance is often a precursor to medical treatment for those who are underinsured or uninsured. For those without adequate insurance coverage, there is a correlation with overall negative health outcomes for children. "Given the importance of public health insurance for this population of children, the current economic realities and threatening state budget cuts pose potentially serious implications for their care, especially for those who rely on public insurance" (McGrath et. al., p. 448).

Identifying the Gaps

Despite the ability to identify ASD symptoms as early as 18 months, data show that some children are not being diagnosed with ASD until they are of school age (Palmer, Blanchard, Jean, & Mandell, 2005). Researchers report more than 75% of children with ASDs are identified through the school system (Boyle et al., 2011) despite variations on how educational criteria are applied at the state level (Barton et al., 2016). Further, these children are four times more likely to receive comprehensive services in school settings which include academic accommodations as well as other supplemental support (i.e., speech language therapy, occupational therapy, social skills, and behavioral therapy) than children with non-ASD diagnoses (Mandell et al., 2005).

Determining the most efficient routes to diagnosis is critical for capitalizing on the opportunities to find families, children in need, and provide best-practice care. Providing education and training to parents regarding how to effectively and efficiently access services, (Bearss, Burrell, Stewart, & Scahill, 2015) would help to address parent stress related to their child's disability status (Woodman, 2014). However, prior to making recommendations, it is important to document how and where parents are accessing diagnostic and intervention services. Also, if there are differences in the pathway to care that are based on parent poverty status, this suggests that education efforts and outreach will require tailored materials. Based on the above conclusions, we seek to answer the following questions: a) For parents of children with ASDs, does poverty status predict diagnosis-seeking behavior, age when the child was diagnosed, or steps (pathway) to diagnosis? b) Is there any relationship between health care access and type or total services used (i.e., behavioral interventions, occupational therapies, social skills training, and sensory integration) and child poverty level? c) Is level of poverty related to the type of healthcare providers working with children with ASDs? d) Is there a difference between under and above FPL group in terms of satisfaction regarding quality of service outcomes?

Methods

Data

Data used in this study were from the 2011 Survey of Pathways to Diagnosis and Services (commonly referred to as Pathways; SPDS), which is a follow-up to the 2009-2010 National Survey of Children with Special Health Care Needs (NS-CSHCN). The SPDS is a nationally representative sample of children ages 6 to 17 years old with special health care needs and a diagnosis of an autism spectrum disorder, intellectual disability, or developmental delay.

Pathways used a telephone interview ($N = 4,032$) and a self-administered questionnaire ($N = 3,997$) where parents and guardians were asked about the emergence of their child's symptoms, the context of the original diagnoses, which providers made the diagnoses, the child's current diagnostic status, the types of clinical treatments/interventions and educational services used to address the developmental problems, as well as other parental concerns or perspectives about their child's behavior, strengths, and difficulties in addition to demographic data including income level and poverty status. This data set provides a unique opportunity to examine which evidence-based services (e.g., speech and language therapy, behavioral intervention, social skill training, occupational therapy, and sensory integration therapy) are provided to children.

Participants

The sample for the present study is a subset of the *Pathways* participants (*N* = 4,032) that were diagnosed with ASDs. This included children who were diagnosed with ASD only, ASD and intellectual disabilities, ASD and other developmental delays, and ASD with intellectual disabilities and developmental delays. In the sample, children with ASDs (*n* = 1725) were separated into two groups; those above FPL, referred to as "above FPL", (*n* = 1477, 85.6%) and "below FPL" (*n* = 248, 14.4%). The actual analytical sample for multivariable linear and logistic regression models varied slightly because of valid non-response to some dependent variables.

Procedure

After obtaining university Institutional Review Board approval and the permission to use the data set from the National Institute of Mental Health (NIMH), the data set was narrowed to focus upon two primary independent variables: all participants with a diagnosis of ASD and families who met the definition of below or above the FPL.

Measures

Pre-screening of data was conducted to identify any outliers and missing data, and to collapse the response categories of the independent variables where there were small sample sizes. For example, for the variable "race," the categories of "black only" and "other race" in the original data were combined into one category "minority." The *Pathways* data categorize poverty status into 4 levels related to FPL: 0 - 99%, 100 - 199%, 200 - 399%, and greater than 400%. As such, the poverty variable data 0 - 99% of FPL are denoted as the "under FPL" group, and data over 100% poverty (i.e., 100 - 199%, 200 - 399%, and greater than 400%) were combined in to the "above FPL" group.

Dependent variables. The main dependent variables were "health care and educational services use," which included, "diagnostic service and intervention" and "treatment services."

Diagnostic services. The diagnostic services variables included parents' diagnosis seeking behavior, the pathway to obtaining a diagnosis of ASD, and age of the diagnosis. (A). *Diagnosis seeking behavior* is measured by the total score parents indicated were an area of concern, which led them to seek a diagnosis for their child. Potential areas of concern included their child's language, social, emotional, and cognitive development, and their attempt to get answers for their concern.

(B). *Pathway to diagnosis* is measured by analyzing the processes parents took to gain diagnosis for their child. It includes questions about health care providers' responses to their diagnosis seeking behavior, school professionals' response to their concern, types of healthcare providers, and other professionals parents contacted to get a formal diagnosis, and their level of involvement in the diagnosis process (e.g., complete a questionnaire, provide opportunity to express their concern to the professional). (C). *Age of diagnosis* measures the age when each child is formally diagnosed.

Intervention and treatment services. These are questions about the current intervention and treatment services that children are receiving including behavioral interventions, occupational therapy, social skills training and sensory integration, language and speech therapy, among others. In addition, parents' self-reported satisfaction of the services their child received in health care and educational services is measured.

Independent variable. The independent variable was the child's poverty status defined in the survey as either "under FPL" or "above FPL."

Covariates. A range of demographic variables (parent/families and child variables) is included as covariates in the multivariate linear and logistic regression models. Covariates included a measure of parental education (less than high school graduate compared with high school graduate or higher); the child's race (white or minority); whether the family lives in an urban area, which is a proxy indicator of proximity to available services; insurance coverage (child had public health insurance compared with privately insured children); and having a regular source of care (early intervention plan, health care service).

Analysis

Chi-square analysis, descriptive bivariate analysis, and multivariate analysis were performed to examine the relationship that poverty has with access and utilization of health care and educational services as well as to see the difference between the two FPL groups. Specifically, independent t-tests were used to determine if there were differences between the below FPL and above FPL groups in their diagnosis seeking behaviors, age when the child was diagnosed, and responses from healthcare and school professionals to the diagnosis. Chi-square analyses were used to determine if there was a statistical difference in the distribution of each service variable (e.g., having a specialty care service such as behavioral intervention, language and speech therapy, occupational therapy, social skill training, and sensory integration therapy) by the binary (poverty) dependent measures. For the continuous dependent measure (number of specialty care services), an estimated linear regression model and bivariate linear regression analysis with a Wald Test was used to obtain adjusted F-ratios.

Results

Demographic data, poverty status, and clinical characteristics beyond the diagnosis of ASD are presented in Table 1. There was a statistically significant difference between the two FPL groups related to the families' level of education and living in an urban setting. Participants under FPL tended to have a low level of education and were more likely to live in urban settings than their above FPL counterparts. However, there were no differences between FPL groups regarding the child's age of diagnosis, child treatment needs, insurance coverage or severity of child's condition when comparing the under FPL group and the above FPL group. A chi-square analysis was conducted to investigate differences in the types of schools attended by the different FPL groupings.

The chi-square analysis indicated a significant difference between the FPL groupings and the types of schools attended by the children with ASD, χ^2 (2, 1497) = 11.056, p < 0.004. Specifically, 91.9% of children in the under FPL group go to public school, whereas only 86.2% of children from the above FPL group attend public school. 2.8% of children below FPL and 9.1% of the children above FPL attended private schools, and 5.3% of children below FPL and 4.7% of children above FPL were home-schooled. These results indicated that those under FPL were more likely to attend public school than their above FPL counterparts; those under FPL were also more likely to be home-schooled than their above FPL counterparts; and those above FPL were more likely to attend private school than those who fell into the under FPL category. Though not significant, the differences in child ages among poverty levels were as follows: 52.4% of children below FPL and 50.1% of children above FPL were 6-11 years old, and 47.6% of children under FPL and 49.9% of children above FPL were 12-17 years old. Differences in gender in relation to poverty levels were not significant and can be described as follows: 76.6% of children under FPL and 79.7% of children above FPL were male, and 23.4% of children below FPL and 20.3% of children above FPL were female. Finally, a chi-square analysis was conducted to investigate differences in race among the poverty level groups. Results indicated a significant difference between the FPL groupings in terms of race, χ^2 (1, 1368) = 47.780, p < 0.001. Specifically, 63.2%

of children under FPL and 82.5% of children above FPL were white, and 36.8% of children under FPL and 17.5% of children above FPL were minorities. These results indicated that there is a significant difference between the FPL groups in terms of race. The above FPL group was more frequently associated with white individuals than minorities, and the under FPL was more frequently associated with minorities than whites.

Research Question #1

For parents of children with ASDs, does poverty status predict diagnostic-seeking behavior, age when the child was diagnosed, or steps (pathway) to diagnosis?

Diagnosis seeking behavior. To examine whether poverty predicts diagnosis-seeking behavior of parents of children with ASD, an independent samples t-test was conducted. To determine if there were differences in the type or number (total) of concerns parents had that resulted in their diagnosis-seeking behaviors, t-test analysis was used to compare the two groups (based on FPL status) on a variety of parent concerns (e.g., medical, cognitive, behavioral, language and communication, and social). Results indicated that there were significant differences in all developmental areas categories, with the exception of social, between the under FPL and the above FPL categories.

Specifically, regarding medical concerns (e.g., having seizures), the under FPL group ($M = 4.59$, $SD = 1.00$) and above FPL group ($M = 4.91$, $SD = 1.02$), were statistically different, $t(1,127) = -3.842$, $p < .001$, indicating that those with a higher SES had more medical concerns related to their child than participants in the lower SES category. For the cognitive concern category (e.g., difficulty learning), the lower FPL group ($M = 5.23$, $SD = 1.28$) and above FPL group ($M = 5.98$, $SD = 1.55$) were statistically different, $t(1,127) = -6.81$, $p < .001$, indicating that those with a higher SES communicated cognitive concerns related to their children more often than those with a lower SES.

Table 1:
Demographic and Clinical Characteristics of Participants (N= 1725)

Characteristics		Under FPL (n=248) % or M (SD)	Above FPL (n=1477) % or M (SD)	Test statistic F
Parent education	High school graduate or less	52	5	8.017**
	More than high school graduate	45	95	
Residences	Urban setting	62	38	9.94**
	Non-urban setting	30	62	
Clinical characteristics of the child	Age of diagnosis	1.94(0.78)	1.9 (0.78)	0.867
	Child needs treatment for emotional development or behavioral problem	78	76	3.042
	child constantly affected	72	75	0.08
	Receiving public insurance	38	31	0.06
Type of school the child currently enrolled	Public	91.9	86.2	11.056**
	Private	2.8	9.1	
	Home-schooled	5.3	4.7	
Age of child in Pathways survey	6-11 years old	52.4	50.1	.456
	12-17 years old	47.6	49.9	
Sex of the child	Male	76.6	79.9	1.210
	Female	23.4	20.3	
Race of the child	White	63.2	82.5	47.780**
	Minority	36.8	17.5	

Note: *p < 0.05, ** P < .01

For the language and communication category, there was a significant difference between under FPL ($M = 6.97$, $SD = 1.66$) and the above FPL groups ($M = 7.77$, $SD = 1.86$), t (1,127) – 3.218, $p = .001$. Continuing with the trend, the higher SES communicated concern related to their child's language and communication more often than the lower SES group. The diagnosis-seeking behavior of parents related to their child's behavioral concerns also differed significantly between the above FPL group ($M = 4.11$, $SD = .97$) and the under FPL group ($M = 3.72$, $SD = 1.06$), t (1,127) = -4.63, $p < .001$, indicating that those in the above FPL category had significantly more concerns related to their child's behavior than those in the lower SES group. Finally, the social concern category was not significantly different ($p = .30$) between the under FPL group ($M = 2.44$, $SD = .78$) and the FPL group ($M = 2.57$, $SD = .74$).

Parents' pathway to an ASD diagnosis for their child. The parents' experience obtaining the initial ASD diagnosis for their child was measured through the context of: a) health care providers' level of responses to parent diagnostic seeking behaviors, b) school professionals' level of responses to parents' diagnostic seeking behaviors, and c) the number and type of professionals involved in the diagnostic process using crosstab and t-test analysis.

When considering the level of responses from health care providers and school professionals to their diagnostic seeking behavior, the t-test analysis yielded significant differences, t (1460) = 3.958, $p < .001$ between the under FPL group ($M = 1.86$, $SD = 2.04$) and the above FPL group ($M = 1.37$, $SD = 1.58$). This indicated that the above FPL parents received a higher number of responses from health professionals during the diagnostic services compared to the under FPL group. Regarding parents' experience of school professionals' responses to their concerns (i.e., diagnosis seeking behavior), the t-test result yielded a significant difference between parents with under FPL ($M = 2.79$, $SD = 2.6$)

Table 2:
Group Description of Diagnosis-seeking Behavior by the Child's Developmental Areas

Help-seeking behavior	Group	Mean	SD	N
Medical	Parents Under FPL	4.59	1.05	152
	Parents Above FPL	4.917	1.025	977
Cognitive	Parents Under FPL	5.23	1.29	152
	Parents Above FPL	5.98	1.55	977
Behavioral	Parents Under FPL	3.72	1.06	152
	Parents Above FPL	4.11	.977	977
Language & communication	Parents Under FPL	6.97	1.66	168
	Parents Above FPL	7.77	1.86	1069
Social	Parents Under FPL	2.44	.78	152
	Parents Above FPL	2.57	.743	977

and parents with above FPL ($M = 2.37$, $SD = 2.4$), t (1452) = 2.252, $p = 0.024$ indicating that the under FPL group received more for their concern from school professionals compared to the above FPL group.

Age of diagnosis. Independent samples t-tests were also used to ascertain whether poverty predicts the age in which children are diagnosed with autism. The t-tests yielded no statistically significant results between the below poverty level ($M = 1.90$, $SD = .303$) and the above poverty groups ($M = 1.90$, $SD = .303$), t (1510) =.021, $p = 0.984$), indicating that age was not different at the time of diagnosis.

Table 3:
Service Providers' Responses to Parents' Diagnosis-Seeking Behavior

Variable	Group	Mean	SD	N
Health care providers' responses to parents' concern	Under FPL group	1.3753	1.584	215
	Above FPL group	1.8605	2.045	1247
School professionals' responses to parents' concern	Under FPL group	2.7905	2.627	210
	Above FPL group	2.3762	2.437	1244
Number of professionals involved in the diagnosis process	Under FPL group	2.1417	6.491	120
	Above FPL group	2.6172	8.515	708

Research Question #2

Is there any relationship between health care access and type or total services used (i.e., behavioral interventions, occupational therapies, social skills training and sensory integration) and child poverty level?

A one-way analysis of variance compared poverty status groups on type of interventions currently provided to the children diagnosed with ASD. See Table 4 for a results summary. There were no statistically significant differences in behavioral, sensory integration therapy, social skill training, and speech and language therapy between the under FPL and above FPL groups. However, there was a significant difference for the cognitive ($F_{(1, 1569)} = 4.287$, $p = 0.039$) and occupational therapy ($F_{(1, 1691)} = 19.4$, $p = 0.001$) services. Results also yielded a significant difference in the number of specialty services that children received

$(F\ (1;\ 1723) = 12.4, p = 0.01)$. This meant that children from above FPL group ($M = 2.75$, $SD = 1.95$) were more likely to receive a larger number of specialty services (e.g., behavioral intervention, cognitive therapy, speech and language therapy, occupational therapy, sensory integration, etc.) than children from under FPL group ($M = 2.36$, $SD = 1.85$)

Table 4:
Currently Receiving Intervention by Level of Poverty (N = 1725)

Outcome variables	Under FPL (n=371)	Above FPL (n=1354)	Test statistic
	M (SD)	M (SD)	F
Currently receiving behavioral intervention	1.61(0.48)	1.66(0.47)	2.717
Currently receiving sensory integration therapy	1.78 (.41)	1.81 (.39)	2.32
Currently receiving cognitive therapy	1.70 (.45)	1.76 (.42)	4.287*
Currently receiving occupational therapy (school based or other)	1.47 (.50)	1.60 (.49)	19.4 **
Currently receiving social skills training (school based or other)	1.41 (.49)	1.44 (.49)	1.06
Currently receiving speech or language therapy (school based or other)	1.44 (.49)	1.49 (.50)	2.38
Number of specialty services	2.36 (1.85)	2.75 (1.95)	12.4**

*Note. *$p < 0.05$ ** $P < 0.01$*

Research Question #3

Is level of poverty related to the type of healthcare providers working with children with ASDs?

To determine if poverty status was related to the type of health care provider options, a chi-square analysis was used to compare the type of provider (e.g., audiologist, developmental pediatrician, neurologist, nurse, pediatrician, primary care practitioner, psychiatrist, psychologist (non-school), school psychologist or counselor, physical, occupational, speech, or other therapist) who was currently working with the child on a regular basis with the child's poverty status. See Table 5 for full results.

The frequency of children from the above FPL group who were currently working with an *audiologist* was 61.5%, whereas the frequency of those children from under poverty group was only 38.5% The difference in frequency is significant at χ^2 (1, N = 65) = 12.062, p < 0.001. The frequency of children from the above FPL group who were currently working with *developmental pediatricians* on a regular basis was 71.2%, whereas the frequency of those children from the under FPL group was only 28.8%. The difference in frequency is significant at χ^2 (1, N = 236) = 8.557, p < 0.003. The frequency of children from the above FPL group who were currently working with a *neurologist* on a regular basis was 72.2%, whereas the frequency of those children from the under FP group was only 27.8 %. The difference in frequency is significant, χ^2 (1, N = 205) = 5.863, p < 0.015. The frequency of children from the above FPL group who were currently working with a *nutritionist* on a regular basis was 62%, whereas the frequency of those children from the under FPL group was only 38%. The difference in frequency is significant at χ^2 (1, N = 92) = 15.704, p < 0.001. The frequency of children from above FPL group who currently work with a *psychiatrist* on a regular basis was 73.1%, whereas the frequency of those children from the under FPL group was only 26.9%. The difference in frequency is significant, χ^2 (1, N = 494) = 11.955, p < 0.001.

The frequency of children from the above FPL group who were currently work with a psychologist or psychotherapist on a regular basis was 74.3%, whereas the frequency of those children from the under FPL group was only 25.7%. The difference in frequency is significant, χ^2 (1, N = 443) = 7.501, p < 0.006.

Table 5:
Type of Healthcare Providers Working with the Child with ASD

Type of healthcare provider working with the child with ASD	Under FPL (*n*=371)	Above FPL (*n*=1354)	Test statistic
	N (%)	N (%)	χ^2
Audiologist	25 (38.5)	40 (61.5)	12.062**
Developmental pediatrician	68 (28.8)	168 (71.2)	8.557*
Neurologist	57 (27.8)	148 (72.2)	5.863*
Nutritionist	57 (62)	35 (38)	15.704**
Psychiatrist	133 (26.9)	361 (73.1)	11.955**
Psychologist or psychotherapist	114 (25.7)	329 (74.3)	7.501*

*Note. *p* < 0.05 ** P < 0.01*

Research Question #4

Is there a difference between under and above FPL group in terms of satisfaction regarding quality of service outcomes?

To investigate parents' perception and satisfaction of the quality of services received on their pathway to a diagnosis for their child, a multivariate test was used to determine if there were significant differences between the two FPL groups in terms of parent's level of satisfaction related to receiving diagnostic services, Pillai's Trace = .008, F = 4.486, df = (3, 1696), p = .004. Specifically, tests of between-subjects effects yielded significant differences between parents with below FPL level and parents with above FPL levels for the items asking if parents agreed: the doctors and other healthcare providers meet the needs of their child, $F(1, 1,098) = 8.351$, $p = .004$, and parents are satisfied with the services that their child receives from doctors and other health care providers, $F(1, 1,698) = 12.362$, $p < .001$. This shows a difference in satisfaction; parents with high SES reported more satisfaction with the services they received than parents with low SES.

Discussion

The results of this study show that families below the FPL are significantly more likely to be of minority status, have less education, and live in urban settings. Children are more likely to attend public school or be homeschooled than attend a private school when compared to families 100% and higher than the FPL. Interestingly, there were no differences in the children's treatment needs, severity of the condition, or insurance status based on FPL. These results highlight why poverty has been described as an independent and clinically meaningful contributor affecting families of children with ASD risk factor throughout the literature.

In regards to parents' approach to seeking a diagnosis, children from higher SES families communicated significantly more concerns related to their child's behavior than families below the FPL. Specifically, families above the FPL were concerned about medical, cognitive, language and communication, but not social issues in their child's development. Although there was no difference in the age of the child when they were diagnosed, families above the FPL were more likely to find health care providers responsive to their needs whereas families below the FPL were more likely to find school professionals responsive to their needs. These results are consistent with previous research showing the higher SES families may be alert to warning signs and keep regularly scheduled visits with heath care providers (Birenbaum, 2002) and as such, have more access to health providers. Data showing that schools were the primary responders to families below the FPL is consistent with the charge that school districts are required to find children in need (20 U.S.C. 1412 a (3)) and provide care whereas there is no such mandate for health care providers. Indeed, poor families may not be aware of services they could access through health care coverage (Enwefa et al., 2006). Given that age of diagnosis was not different between the groups, this lends support to the conclusion that there is an increased awareness of ASD symptoms across many service delivery personnel and systems.

These data also show that the higher SES families were accessing more comprehensive care services that is in line with Longtin and Principe's (2014) findings that higher SES parents were more aware of the services that their children received. Presumably, parents that are accessing more services are also aware of their services available to their children. Specifically, these higher SES families indicate seeking services from audiologists, developmental pediatricians, neurologists, nutritionists, psychiatrists, and psychologists or psychotherapists significantly more often than families below the FPL. Importantly, these families were also more satisfied with their services than the families below the FPL.

Taken altogether, the data from this study provide a unique perspective into the effects of poverty because the variables that were not different (e.g., age of diagnosis, child treatment needs, severity of the condition or insurance status) may have explained why parents would report more concerns, or why health care or school care would be initiated. Instead, these data support previous studies showing that it is the effects of poverty that often result in a lack of exposure to opportunities, inequality in service delivery and differences in approaches to managing social problems (Enwefa et al., 2006). These results are a call to action for all service providers serving families where ASDs are present.

Conclusion and Implications

School systems are likely to have the most opportunity to communicate with families below the FPL about how to access health services alongside school-based services for children with ASD. As such, school communications should be prioritized and tailored to poor families. Communications with families could coincide with the well-established *Child Find* (20 U.S.C. 1412 a (3)) activities that occur, at least, annually. Educational materials would need to be similar to those provided to at-risk families regarding *Head Start* and other educational supports (Breitenstein et. al., 2007). Providing and coordinating integrated care services is a typical role for school districts, particularly when a child has a disability such as ASD requiring special education services. Schools may seek to use established partnerships (e.g., school-based health centers) or reach out to local providers based on the child's needs, family poverty level, and local customs to address gaps that exist for families below FPL.

Health care providers treating children through CHIP and Medicaid should ensure that they have adequate outreach efforts to support families with children who may have ASD. The American Academy of Pediatrics has guidelines for the recognition and treatment of ASDs including a toolkit for health care providers (Liptak et al., 2008). The toolkit explains the need for routine screenings for all children, and how to establish a network of community based resources that can link to early intervention services for all families.

Although research has shown that integrated care is effective for children with ASD in well-coordinated systems, like the Medical Home (Davis & Homan, 2015), researchers need to establish protocols for determining the usefulness of broad based, public outreach that is appropriate for impoverished families. One promising model is the Act Early Regional Summit Project, which studied state-based initiatives focused on increasing awareness, education and training, and policy change for the early diagnosis and intervention of children with ASDs. The program is one of the first of its kind to look at how development of comprehensive state plans and engagement of key stakeholders can foster positive outcomes in early intervention services for children with ASD (Peacock & Lin, 2012). Results from the model emphasize the importance of coordinating services across care categories (e.g., pediatricians, mental health providers, developmental specialists, and therapists) in order to reach children from all racial, ethnic, geographic, and socioeconomic backgrounds. However, still missing from these programs are efforts to reach and include parents, particularly those who are impoverished and have low access to information, as informed partners. Supporting parent stress management and pathways for participation is a call to action for health care and school providers. Parent-school-community partnerships are essential for this success.

Author's Note:

Correspondence regarding this article should be addressed to Waganesh Zeleke, Ed.D, LCPC, NCC, Assistant Professor, Department of Counseling, Psychology, and Special Needs Education, Duquesne University, 110E Canevin Hall, 600 Forbes Ave., Pittsburgh, PA, 15282; Tel: (412)396-2465; e-mail: zelekew@duq.edu.

References

Barton, E. E., Harris, B., Leech, N., Stiff, L., Choi, G., & Joel, T. (2016). An analysis of state autism educational assessment practices and requirements. *Journal of Autism and Developmental Disorders, 46*, 737-748.

Bearss, K., Burrell, T. L., Stewart, L., & Scahill, L. (2015). Parent training in autism spectrum disorder: What's in a name? *Clinical Child and Family Psychology Review, 18*, 170-182.

Birenbaum, A. (2002). Poverty, welfare reform, and disproportionate rates of disability among children. *Mental Retardation, 40*, 212-218.

Bitterman, A., Daley, T. C., Misra, S., Carlson, E., & Markowitz, J. (2008). A national sample of preschoolers with autism spectrum disorders: Special education services and parent satisfaction. *Journal of Autism and Developmental Disorders, 38,* 1509-1517.

Boyle, C. A., Boulet, S., Schieve, L. A., Cohen, R. A., Blumberg, S. J., Yeargin-Allsopp, M., & Kogan, M. D. (2011). Trends in the prevalence of developmental disabilities in US children, 1997–2008. *Pediatrics, 127,* 1034-1042.

Bradley, R. H., & Corwyn, R. F. (2002). Socioeconomic status and child development. *Annual Review of Psychology, 53,* 371-399.

Breitenstein, S. M., Gross, D., Ordaz, I., Julion, W., Garvey, C., & Ridge, A. (2007). Promoting mental health in early childhood programs serving families from low-income neighborhoods. *Journal of the American Psychiatric Nurses Association, 13,* 313-320.

Center for Disease Control and Prevention (2016). *New data on autism: Five facts to know.* Retrieved from https://www.cdc.gov/features/new-autism-data/index. html

Children's Defense Fund (2017). *Children's Health.* Retrieved from http://www. childrensdefense.org/policy/health

Davis, A. M., & Homan, S. (2015). *Meeting healthcare needs of children with autism spectrum disorders: Family centered medical home matters.* Retrieved from http://digitalcommons.hsc.unt.edu/rad/RAD15/GeneralPublicHealth/20

Enwefa, R. L., Enwefa, S. C., & Jennings, R. (2006). Special education: Examining the impact of poverty on the quality of life of families of children with disabilities. *Forum on Public Policy,* 1-27.

Ferguson, H. B., Bovaird, S., & Mueller, M. P. (2007). The impact of poverty on educational outcomes for children. *Pediatrics & Child Health, 12,* 701.

Fujiura, G. T., & Yamaki, K. (2000). Trends in demography of childhood poverty and disability. *Exceptional Children, 66,* 187-199.

Hume, K., Bellini, S., & Pratt, C. (2005). The usage and perceived outcomes of early intervention and early childhood programs for young children with autism spectrum disorder. *Topics in Early Childhood Special Education, 25,* 195–207.

Individuals with Disabilities Education Improvement Act, 20 U.S.C. § 1400 (2004).

Ingersoll, B., & Dvortcsak, A. (2006). Including parent training in the early childhood special education curriculum for children with autism spectrum disorders. *Journal of Positive Behavior Interventions, 8,* 79-87.

Jensen, E. (2009). How poverty affects behavior and academic performance. In *Teaching with poverty in mind (2)*. Retrieved from http://www.ascd.org/publications/books/109074/chapters/How-Poverty-Affects-Behavior-and-Academic-Performance.aspx

KewalRamani, A. (2007). *Status and trends in the education of racial and ethnic minorities.* Retrieved from http://files.eric.ed.gov/fulltext/ED498259.pdf

Kochanska, G., & Aksan, N. (1995). Mother-child mutually positive affect, the quality of child compliance to requests and prohibitions, and maternal control as correlates of early internalization. *Child Development, 66,* 236–254.

Li-Grining, C. P., & Durlak, J. A. (2014). The design and implementation of early childhood intervention programs: Informing efforts to address risk and promote resilience. *Journal of Prevention & Intervention in the Community, 42,* 243-247.

Liptak, G. S., Benzoni, L. B., Mruzek, D. W., Nolan, K. W., Thingvoll, M. A., Wade, C. M., & Fryer, G. E. (2008). Disparities in diagnosis and access to health services for children with autism: Data from the National Survey of Children's Health. *Journal of Developmental & Behavioral Pediatrics, 29,* 152-160.

Longtin, S. E., & Principe, G. M. (2014). The relationship between poverty level and urban African American parents' awareness of evidence-based interventions for children with autism spectrum disorders: Preliminary data. *Focus on Autism and Other Developmental Disabilities, 31,* 83-91.

Mandell, D. S., Morales, K. H., Xie, M., Lawer, L. J., Stahmer, A. C., & Marcus, S. C. (2010). Age of diagnosis among Medicaid-enrolled children with autism, 2001-2004. *Psychiatric Services, 61,* 822-829.

Mandell, D. S., Novak, M. M., & Zubritsky, C. D. (2005). Factors associated with age of diagnosis among children with autism spectrum disorders. *Pediatrics, 116,* 1480-1486.

McGrath, R. J., Laflamme, D. J., Schwartz, A. P., Stransky, M., & Moeschler, J. B. (2009). Access to genetic counseling for children with autism, down syndrome, and intellectual disabilities. *Pediatrics, 124,* 443-449.

National Institute for Health Care Management. (2008). *Understanding the uninsured: Tailoring policy solutions for different subpopulations.* Retrieved from https://www.nihcm.org/pdf/NIHCM-Uninsured-Final.pdf

National Research Council. (2001). Educating children with autism. In C. Lord & J. P. McGee, Committee on educational interventions for children with autism. Washington, DC: National Academy Press, Division of Behavioral and Social Sciences and Education.

Owens, E. B., & Shaw, D. S. (2003). Poverty and early childhood adjustment. In S. S. Luthar (Ed), *Resilience and Vulnerability: Adaptation in the Context of Childhood Adversities, 267*-292. Cambridge, England: Cambridge University Press.

Palmer, R. F., Blanchard, S., Jean, C. R., & Mandell, D. S. (2005). School district resources and identification of children with autistic disorder. *American Journal of Public Health, 95,* 125-130.

Patient Protection and Affordable Care Act, 42, U.S.C. § 18001 (2010).

Peacock, G., Amendah, D., Ouyang, L., & Grosse, S. D. (2012). Autism spectrum disorders and health care expenditures: The effects of co-occurring conditions. *Journal of Developmental & Behavioral Pediatrics, 33,* 2-8.

Peacock, G., & Lin, S. C. (2012). Enhancing early identification and coordination of intervention services for young children with autism spectrum disorders: Report from the Act Early Regional Summit Project. *Disability and Health Journal, 5,* 55-59.

Pennsylvania House of Representatives Major Policy Committee (2014). Beyond poverty: Preliminary findings from the 2013-2014 empowering opportunities: Gateways out of poverty initiative.

Rogers, S. (1996). Brief report: Early intervention in autism. *Journal of Autism and Developmental Disorders, 26,* 243–246.

Schulzinger, R., Haifley, G., & Allen, M., (2003). Action strategies and resource guide: Promoting children's mental health screens and assessments. Children's Defense Fund.

Semansky, R. M., Xie, M., & Mandell, D. S. (2011). Datapoints: Medicaid's increasing role in treating youths with autism spectrum disorders. *Psychiatric Services, 62,* 588.

Sirin, S. R. (2005). Socioeconomic status and academic achievement: A meta-analytic review of research. *Review of Educational Research, 75,* 417-453.

Skiba, R. J., Poloni-Staudinger, L., Simmons, A. B., Feggins-Azziz, L. R., & Chung, C. G. (2005). Unproven links can poverty explain ethnic disproportionality in special education? *The Journal of Special Education, 39,* 130-144.

The Supplemental Poverty Measure: 2015. (2016). Retrieved from http://www.census.gov/content/dam/Census/library/publications/2016/demo/p60-258.pdf

Thomas, K. C., Ellis, A. R., McLaurin, C., Daniels, J., & Morrissey, J. P. (2007). Access to care for autism-related services. *Journal of Autism and Developmental Disorders, 37,* 1902-1912.

U.S. Code Title 42, The Public Health and Welfare, Chapter 106. 42 U.S.C. 9902

United States Department of Health and Human Services. (2015). *Frequently asked questions related to the poverty guidelines and poverty.* Retrieved from https://aspe.hhs.gov/frequently-asked-questions-related-poverty-guidelines-and-poverty#differences.

Woodman, A. C. (2014). Trajectories of stress among parents of children with disabilities: A dyadic analysis. *Family Relations, 63,* 39-54.

Influences of Childcare Quality for Children with Disruptive Behavior Disorders

Sierra L. Brown, Kara E. McGoey, Scott L. Graves, and James B. Schreiber

Abstract

The relationship between childcare type (e.g., public preschool, private, Head Start, childcare, nursery school) and quality indicators (e.g., environmental, teacher-child interaction, and teacher quality) were examined to determine the influence on school readiness for children with disruptive behavior disorders. Results indicated public prekindergarten programs possessed the most indicators of childcare quality by considering the highest rating on the Early Childhood Environment Rating Scale-Revised (ECERS-R), Arnett Caregiver Sensitivity Scale, and teacher's education. Children enrolled in private childcare programs predicted better prosocial skills in kindergarten. Additionally, attendance in Head Start programs also predicted fewer problematic behaviors. Similar to previous research, results suggest that teacher-child relationships significantly predicted fewer problematic behaviors in kindergarten. Academic-related skills in kindergarten were most predicted by teacher-child interactions.

Key Words: childcare, quality indicators, school readiness, disruptive behavior disorders

The participation in childcare settings has increased from 127,000 children in 1965 to nearly 2.7 million in 2009 (Epstein & Barnett, 2012). As more children enter into non-parental care, a major focus of childcare has shifted from daycare for working families to building a capacity for pre-academic skills and ensure readiness for school entry. Education policy in the United States, in particular, has had a specific interest in ensuring quality care and adequate preparation for school readiness skills. For example, No Child Left Behind (No Child Left Behind Act [NCLB], 2002) recognized that many students were delayed at school entry, including students with disabilities, minority students, and students from low socioeconomic backgrounds. NCLB responded to the need of quality education for elementary and secondary school students in order to close the achievement gap. However, school readiness skills are developed well before elementary school and many are children from disadvantaged backgrounds.

What is School Readiness?

Traditionally, school readiness is considered to be mastery of pre-academic skills (i.e., language and literacy skills, basic numerical skills, and general knowledge). However, social-emotional development including social skills, emotional knowledge and control, and behavioral control is also considered an integral part of school readiness (Mehaffie & Fraser, 2007). Social-emotional development is vital for preschool as children need to develop age-appropriate behavioral control in order to learn the pre-academic concepts necessary for school entry. Interestingly, caregivers and teachers differ in opinions of what is important for school readiness. Parents rated academic readiness skills as essential to kindergarten entry whereas preschool and kindergarten teachers endorsed social-emotional development as the highest priority for school readiness (Piotrkowski, Botsko, & Matthews, 2001). In short, teachers felt prepared to teach academic skills that may be delayed, but they believed it was essential for children to enter school with social-emotional skills so that children would be ready to benefit from the academic material.

Childcare and Academic Outcomes

The effect of the time spent in non-parental care has been an important concern. For example, there is an extensive research base examining the effects of quality childcare attendance on a child's development which has produced mixed results where both positive and negative effects have been shown on academic achievement (Li, Farkas, Duncan, Burchinal, & Vandell, 2013; Mashburn et al., 2008; National Institute of Child Health and Human Development [NICHD], 2002). The research showing that the largest negative impact on the time spent in childcare was dependent on the quality of the childcare setting. Similarly, childcare quality has a significant moderating factor that has been shown to influence academic gains for preschoolers. Several studies indicated that academic gains tended to be larger for children who attended higher quality programs than those who attended low quality programs. Additionally, quality programs contributed to more significant gains for children from low socioeconomic backgrounds than children from higher socioeconomic backgrounds (Peisner-Feinberg et al., 2001; Votruba-Drzal, Coley, & Chase-Lansdale, 2004).

One factor consistent throughout the literature is that the quality of center-based care can be a unique predictor of school readiness and academic outcomes. Quality can be measured through many different variables, Epstein and Barnett (2012) identify several key factors in the assessment of center-based quality including staff experience and education, type of curriculum implemented, teacher and child interactions, physical environment of the center, program structure, and even the amount of monthly fees. These variables alone are not sufficient to assess the quality of the care, but taken together can provide a basis for quality estimation. There are several factors to evaluate the quality of a childcare center, but data point to instructional quality and teacher characteristics as unique factors that predict academic gains in preschool. Burchinal, Vandergrift, Pianta, & Mashburn (2010) also found that pre-academic skills (e.g., pre-reading, language, and numeracy skills) were uniquely predicted by instructional skills of the classroom teacher. Specifically, teacher education (e.g., possessing at least a bachelors degree) predicted higher receptive vocabulary (Burchinal, Cryer, Clifford, & Howes, 2002).

Childcare attendance has a significant and positive impact on expressive and receptive language development, reading, and math skills (Keys et al., 2013; Peisner-Feinberg et al., 2001; Welsh, Nix, Blair, Bierman, & Nelson, 2010). These findings are particularly salient for children from low-income families. Analyses of programs, such as the Perry Preschool Project, the Carolina Abecedarian Project, and Head Start, demonstrated positive academic gains for children aimed specifically at improving school readiness skills for low-income children (Campbell & Pungello, 2007; Rose, 2010; Weikart, Deloria, Lawser, & Wiegerink, 1970; Zigler & Styfco, 2003). Each of the longitudinal studies found significant academic and cognitive improvements for the children enrolled in the programs three years after the preschool program. Unfortunately, academic and cognitive gains were not shown for children in these programs into elementary school (Campbell & Pungello, 2007; Schweinhart, Barnes, & Weikart, 1993; U.S. Department of Health and Human Services [HHS], 2010; Weikart et al., 1970). Despite these programs showing preschool fadeout, other data suggest that the quality of early education can have a lasting effect on academic functioning in adolescence, suggesting academic achievement was mediated by the quality of the child's early education (Vandell et al., 2010).

Childcare and Social-Emotional Outcomes

Research has demonstrated the importance of quality childcare for academic skills, but quality childcare can be equally important for social-emotional development. Social-emotional development, in particular, fosters age-appropriate peer relations and positive adult-child relationships. In a review of literature on social-emotional development, Raver and Knitzer (2002) noted that children who do not have appropriate social-emotional development are less likely to have peer and teacher acceptance, receive less instruction, and receive less positive feedback from teachers. Thus, these children evidence long-term difficulties, including academic difficulties, grade retention, delinquency, and high school dropout.

Similar to research investigating academic benefits of preschool, quality childcare has a significant impact on social-emotional development. The effects of the time spent in non-parental care on the emotional, social, and behavioral development of young children was an important concern; however, research indicated that the largest negative impact on the time spent in childcare was dependent on the quality of the childcare setting. Research suggested low quality preschool programming had adverse effects for young children both academically and behaviorally (Burchinal et al., 2010; McCartney et al., 2010; NICHD, 2005). Relatedly, longitudinal studies have demonstrated that the positive social-emotional outcomes of high quality programs in childhood lasted into adulthood, including higher graduation rate, lower delinquency, and higher salary. Children who did not receive the high quality programming did not benefit (Heckman, Moon, Pinto, Savelyev, & Yavitz, 2010; Schweinhart et al., 1993; Schweinhart et al., 2005).

As instructional quality is related to academic progress, certain factors also uniquely influence social-emotional development. In a sample of low-income children, Burchinal et al. (2010) found that high quality classrooms with quality teacher-child interaction predicted increased social skills and lower behavior problems than low-quality classrooms. As teacher-child interaction is important for prosocial development, the quality of the relationship between the child and the teacher can influence the perception of behavioral and conduct problems in the preschool classroom. Children with more conflictual relationships with their teachers were more likely to have teachers who reported behavior problems (Graves & Howes, 2011). Research consistently demonstrates the importance of high quality interactions with children that foster social-emotional development.

Low Socioeconomic Status and Quality Preschool

Accessing quality childcare can be cost prohibitive. On average, young children are estimated to attend childcare for 36 hours per week (Epstein & Barnett, 2012). Recent data show that the cost of childcare exceeds that of college tuition in many areas of the United States (Economic Policy Institute [EPI], 2015). Despite the high cost, non-parental childcare is often a necessity for many working parents. For economically disadvantaged families, subsidized childcare may be available, however, these programs are often found to be of lower quality when compared to non-subsidized childcare (Ryan, Johnson, Rigby, & Brooks-Gunn, 2011). Furthermore, higher-quality childcare centers tend not to accept subsidies to cover tuition (Loeb, Fuller, Kagan, & Carrol, 2004). As such, for low-income families, the benefits of attending quality programs are not realized because families do not have adequate access to these programs.

Parents often rely on quality early childhood education to provide young children the opportunity to begin school with the necessary tools to succeed in preschool and beyond. Good programs help to prepare children for formal education with specific pre-academic skills (e.g., pointing to one item at a time) as well as foundational social, emotional, and behavioral development (e.g., responding to your name, following one step directions). When children are not exposed to, or do not develop, these types of pre-requisite skills they can be disadvantaged in performing subsequent preschool expectations (Nix, Bierman, Domitrovich, & Gill, 2013).

Preschool Quality and Disruptive Behaviors

Although there is a large body of research indicating the benefits of quality preschool for children, there is little research available on the impact of quality preschool programming in decreasing behaviors of children with a disruptive behavior disorder [DBD]. Children diagnosed with Attention Deficit/Hyperactivity

Disorder (ADHD) or Oppositional Defiant Disorder (ODD) often lack or have delayed social-emotional skills necessary for proper behavior functioning within the preschool classroom (Campbell, 1994; DuPaul, McGoey, Eckert, & VanBrackle, 2001). Children with DBDs face a multitude of risks for school failure in their preschool years - some of which can be attributed to the childcare environment that can be targeted by quality childcare centers. Preschool programs provide daily structure, routines, and structured peer interactions that are often needed for children with behavior disorders. Thus, it is important to understand the effects of quality preschool on the symptomatology of disruptive behavior disorders.

Children who have externalizing behaviors can continue to struggle throughout their education, leading to academic and continued behavioral difficulties through elementary school and beyond. It is important to target these behaviors early and in a structured, high-quality environment to alleviate or possibly eliminate academic and behavioral difficulties to get children with disruptive behavior disorders ready to succeed in school. Children exhibiting disruptive behaviors become a concern not only because the behaviors interrupt the daily routine of the classroom, but it also puts the child at risk for expulsion or suspension from the preschool setting, which removes the child from educational services that may provide academic benefits for the future. In one study which surveyed 185 teachers, 39.3% of the teachers had expelled at least one preschool child and 14.7% had suspended at least one preschool child, with a higher percentage of teachers expelling children in profit and nonprofit childcare programs than public, private, or Head Start programs (Gilliam & Shahar, 2006). Results of the study also suggest that the expulsion rate for preschoolers exceeded the state's K-12 expulsion rate by 34 times and exceeded the national rate by 13 times (Gilliam & Shahar, 2006). The study identified that the type of program, the class size and age-proportion, as well as teacher-related variables, including stress and depression, was significantly related to preschool expulsion.

Taken altogether, attending quality childcare centers, which has shown to increase behavioral and emotional outcomes, should also, in theory, provide some benefits for children experiencing behavior disorders. These preschool programs have been shown to provide daily structure, routines, and structured peer interactions that are often needed for children with behavior disorders. There is little research available on the impact of quality childcare on decreasing the symptomatology of disruptive behavior disorders. As such, in order to broaden the knowledge base about the potential benefits of preschool programming, it was vital to understand the impact of center-based care for all children, including those with disabilities and disorders that may impede their future academic achievement.

The Present Study

The proposed study incorporates the existing literature and knowledge base to examine the effects of childcare programming on the development of social-emotional skills in children with a DBD. Consequently, the purpose of this study was to examine differences in childcare quality and the impact of quality on social-emotional development. Quality in the current study is determined by examining key variables such as environmental quality (e.g., Early Childhood Environmental Rating Scale-Revised [ECER-R]; Early Childhood Longitudinal Study-Birth Cohort [ECLS-B]), teacher characteristics (e.g., teacher education and experience), and teacher-child interaction as literature indicates that these variables contribute to quality childcare programs and social-emotional development. The current study aims to examine the differences in childcare programs that are identified in the ECLS-B to predict the influence of quality on social-emotional development in preschool. Specifically, the current research seeks to explore the following questions:

1. Do the childcare settings measured in this study (e.g., Head Start, public prekindergarten, preschool/nursery, private, childcare, other) differ on measures of quality (e.g., ECERS-R composite scores, teacher education, teacher experience, teacher-child interaction as measured by the Arnett)?
2. Does the type of childcare center attended (i.e., Head Start, public prekindergarten, preschool/nursery, private, childcare, other) predict the social-emotional development score in kindergarten?

Methods

The following study analyzed data from the ECLS-B dataset. The ECLS-B is a longitudinal dataset that includes a nationally representative sample of approximately 10,700 children born in 2001. Data were collected during five waves of the study: at nine months of age, two years, preschool-age, and in kindergarten during two school years. Information throughout each wave was gathered through interviews and direct child assessments. The current study utilized data from the preschool and 2006 – 2007 kindergarten wave.

Sample

The weighted sample for the main analyses consisted of 20,516 classrooms. Childcare directors were asked to identify the type of center which included public preschool, private center, childcare, Head Start, preschool/nursery, or 'other.' Demographic information of the children included in the sample includes 7,980 female participants and 12,536 males, with a mean age of 66 months. Of the 20,516 participants, 18,894 participants were identified as having DBD symptoms. Diagnosis was determined during the preschool wave via parent report which parents were asked, "Has a doctor ever told you if your child has the following conditions: Oppositional Defiant Disorder and/or ADHD?" Within the sample, 2,090 females were reported to have DBD symptoms compared to 5,978 males. The ethnicity of the participants in the sample included: White, Non-Hispanic ($n = 11,027$), Black or African American, Non-Hispanic ($n = 7,009$), Hispanic ($n = 2,165$), more than one race, Non-Hispanic ($n = 221$).

Measures

Data collection within the ECLS-B included several direct and indirect measures. Specifically, for variables relating to childcare quality (e.g., environmental quality, teacher-child interaction quality, teacher characteristics) and child outcomes, measures included interviews of the childcare providers, structured observations, and kindergarten teacher ratings. These measures were extracted from the ECLS-B database to determine the social-emotional development of the children in kindergarten.

Environmental Quality. To measure the quality of the childcare environment, researchers conducted observations in the preschool settings and completed the ECERS-R (Harms, Clifford, & Cryer, 1998), which is a 43 item rating scale which uses a 1 to 7 rating of the child care environment for children between the ages of 2.5 and 5. The total scaled score of the ECERS-R was used for the analysis of the overall quality of the childcare setting. The data were recoded to reflect the scale of the ECERS-R, where scores from 0 – 2.99 were recoded as "inadequate" settings (0), scores from 3 – 4.99 were recoded as "minimal" (1), scores from 5 – 6.99 were considered "good" (2), and scores of 7 were considered "excellent" (3). Table 1 highlights the weighted totals for ECERS-R by childcare type. The total scale demonstrates an excellent Cronbach's alpha level of 0.95, with subscale Cronbach's alpha levels ranging from 0.83 to 0.92.

Teacher-Child Interaction Quality. The Arnett Caregiver Sensitivity Scale (Arnett, 1989) is a 26 item scale which measures the quality of interactions between teachers and children. Interactions are rated on a 4-point scale ranging from 'not at all' to 'very much' in five domains. A Caregiver Interaction Scale total score provides

Table 1:
Childcare Environmental Quality by Childcare Type

Type	ECERS-R rating			
	Inadequate	Minimally	Good	Total
Public prekindergarten	0	186	2640	2826
Private	1303	1043	1128	3474
Childcare	1417	0	0	1417
Head Start	0	3562	6318	9880
Preschool/nursery	0	1185	1593	2778
Other	66	76	0	142
Total	2786	6052	11679	20517

Note: Totals differ from the analysis due to missing data.

an indication of the overall interaction quality, with scores ranging from 0 to 78. For the purposes of the ECLS-B, the Arnett was slightly modified and items were reworded to provide examples and clarifications for the individual items to improve scoring. The reported Cronbach's alpha for the total Arnett composite score was 0.95 with individual composite Cronbach's alpha levels ranging from 0.80 to 0.95.

Teacher Characteristics. Teachers answered questions about their teaching experience and education in the Early Care and Education Provider (ECEP) telephone interview. For the purposes of the study, variables used in the analysis included total years of education and total years worked in a childcare setting. Data were recoded to reflect a range of years worked in which teachers who reported working five years or less were recoded as 'novice' teachers (0), those who worked between 6 to 10 years were recoded as 'beginner' teachers (1), teachers who worked 11 to 15 years were coded as 'intermediate' (2), and those who worked more than 15 years were coded as 'experienced' (3). Overall, most teachers were considered under the 'beginner' category, having worked in a childcare center between 6 to 10 years. In addition, most of the teachers in the sample reported having a graduate degree. In the current data, teacher education was coded as having less than a high school education (0), high school degree (1), post high school, no degree (2), associates degree (3), bachelor's degree (4), and a graduate degree (5).

Social-Emotional Skills and Behaviors. Parents and preschool teachers completed a measure of social-emotional development based on a modified version of the Preschool and Kindergarten Behavior Scales-Second Edition (PKBS-2; Merrell, 2003) and the Social Skills Rating System (SSRS; Gresham & Elliott, 1990). The ECLS-B modified the PKBS-2 and SSRS to assess constructs of interest (i.e., approaches to learning and friendship). During the administration of the socioemotional skills and behaviors, respondents rated the child's behaviors within the last three months on a 5-point scale ranging from 'never' to 'very often.' Reliability indicators were not reported in the ECLS-B manual as the scale included items from a variety of sources. Three constructs were developed including prosocial skills, problematic behaviors, and academic-related skills.

Results

Descriptive analyses for quality indicators are presented in Table 2. A one-way multivariate analysis of variance (MANOVA) was conducted to determine if there were significant differences in quality (i.e., ECERS-R composite scores and teacher education, teacher experience, and teacher-child interaction as measured by the Arnett) between the type of childcare setting. A Bonferroni correction was used with each ANOVA tested at the 0.0021 level, as 24 comparisons were made (i.e., six types of childcare centers being compared on four indicators of quality). A significant multivariate main effect was observed for childcare programs $F(20, 68012) = 1723$, $p < .001$; Wilks $\Lambda = 0.26$, $\eta p^2 = 0.28$. Significant univariate main effects were observed for ECERS-R scores, $F(5, 20509) = 3687$, $p < .001$, $\eta p^2 = .47$, Arnett scores, $F(5, 20509) = 844$, $p < .001$, $\eta p^2 = 0.17$, the education level of childcare teachers, $F(5,$

Table 2:
Descriptive Statistics of Quality Variables

	N	ECERS-R	Arnett	Education level	Years worked
		M (SD)	M (SD)	M (SD)	M (SD)
Public Prekindergarten	2827	1.93 (0.25)	70.37 (5.67)	5.63 (0.48)	1.70 (0.68)
Private	3473	0.95 (0.84)	63.36 (9.31)	3.09 (1.85)	1.27 (0.55)
Childcare	1417	0.00 (0.00)	55.00 (0.00)	4.00 (0.00)	1.00 (0.00)
Head Start	9879	1.64 (0.48)	65.79 (9.81)	4.41 (0.98)	2.62 (1.36)
Preschool/ nursery	2777	1.57 (0.49)	69.54 (3.44)	5.87 (0.49)	1.61 (0.49)
Other	142	0.54 (0.50)	65.82 (4.50)	3.46 (0.50)	1.46 (0.50)
Total	20515	1.44 (0.72)	65.77 (9.00)	4.52 (1.38)	2.00 (1.19)

20509) $= 2922$, $p < .001$, $\eta p^2 = 0.42$, and the total years childcare teachers worked, $F(5, 20509) = 1504$, $p < .001$, $\eta p^2 = 0.27$.

Results show that public prekindergarten programs were rated the highest on environmental quality on ECERS-R, followed in quality by Head Start programs and preschool/nursery centers. Results showed that overall, childcare centers possessed the fewest quality indicators. However, all of the program types had generally positive interactions with children with mean Arnett scores ranging from 63.4 to 70.4. With regard to teacher education, public prekindergarten and preschool/nursery program teachers typically possessed a bachelor's degree. Though teachers from Head Start programs obtained associate's degrees, they reported more years of experience with generally 6 to 10 years of experience and private preschool teachers reporting the least amount of experience.

Multiple regression analyses were then conducted to determine if quality childcare predicts greater social-emotional development in kindergarten for children with DBD within three domains (e.g., prosocial behaviors, problematic behaviors, and academic-related). Results indicate that the type and quality of childcare significantly predict prosocial skills and account for a significant amount of variance, $R^2 = 0.61$, $R^2_{adj} = 0.61$, $F(11, 9923) = 1416$, $p < .001$. The model accounted for 61% of the variance in prosocial skills when indicators of quality were added to the model. A summary of regression coefficients is presented in Table 3. When examining which variables contribute to higher ratings on prosocial skills, the quality of teacher-child interactions (i.e., Arnett score) is most strongly associated with prosocial skills in kindergarten. Children who attended public prekindergarten were not rated as having the highest prosocial skills compared to children enrolled in childcare settings.

Table 3:
Coefficients for Final Model for Predicting Prosocial Skills

	B	β	t	p	Bivariate r	Partial
Public	.650	.039	5.304	.000	.047	.053
Private	1.152	.420	31.172	.000	.035	.299
Head Start	.513	.267	8.218	.000	.051	.082
Preschool/ nursery	-.225	-.090	-3.587	.000	-.054	-.036
Other	1.299	.118	13.538	.000	-.076	.135
ECERS- inadequate	-2.968	-1.379	-40.143	.000	.003	-.374
ECERS- minimal	-1.509	-.657	-47.371	.000	.050	-.429
Arnett	-.203	-1.631	-116.960	.000	-.339	-.761
Education level	.453	.771	45.995	.000	.061	.419
Years worked	-.164	-.208	-11.542	.000	-.026	-.115
Diagnosis	-.346	-.173	-11.845	.000	-.092	-.118

Next, a regression analysis was conducted to predict the relationship between the classroom, teacher, and child variables for ratings of problematic behaviors. Regression results indicate an overall model which significantly predicts problematic behavior, $R^2 = 0.69$, $R^2adj = 0.69$, $F(11, 9923) = 2078.17$, $p < .001$. The model accounted for 70% of the variance in problematic behaviors. The regression coefficients are presented in Table 4. Compared to children enrolled in childcare, fewer problematic behaviors were predicted by attendance in Head Start. Childcare qualities such as teacher-child interactions predicted less problematic behaviors. In addition, children with DBD symptoms were rated with having more problematic behavior than children who did not show DBD symptoms.

Finally, a regression analysis was conducted to determine the relationship between the independent variables and academic-related skills. Regression results indicate an overall model which significantly predicts problematic behavior, $R^2 = 0.49$, $R^2adj = 0.49$, $F(11, 9923) = 855.46$, $p < .001$. The model accounted for 49% of the variance in academic-related skills. The regression coefficients are presented in Table 5. Children who attended preschool programs were rated as having better academic-related skills compared to children in childcare programs. However, for other indicators of quality, results suggested that teacher-child interactions were related to academic-related skills.

Discussion

The extant literature has identified that quality programs are vital in promoting not only future academic success, but also social-emotional development for children (Burchinal et al., 2010; NICHD, 2005; Peisner-Feinberg et al., 2001). However, these advantages were found in some studies to be dependent on the quality of childcare programs (Burchinal et al., 2010; Magnuson, Ruhm, & Waldfogel, 2007). Determining the construct of "quality" requires consideration of many characteristics of the childcare environment, and one

Table 4:
Coefficients for Final Model for Predicting Problematic Behavior

	B	β	t	p	Bivariate r	Partial
Public	-1.399	-.126	-19.465	.000	-.058	-.192
Private	-.913	-.501	-42.121	.000	-.287	-.389
Head Start	-1.311	-1.026	-35.839	.000	-.095	-.339
Preschool/ nursery	-.740	-.442	-20.094	.000	.054	-.198
Other	-.385	-.052	-6.841	.000	-.003	-.069
ECERS- inadequate	-2.184	-1.527	-50.376	.000	.080	-.451
ECERS-minimal	-.384	-.252	-20.568	.000	-.016	-.202
Arnett	-.126	-1.528	-124.236	.000	-.355	-.780
Education level	.132	.337	22.787	.000	.135	.223
Years worked	-.125	-.239	-15.025	.000	-.044	-.149
Diagnosis	.525	.394	30.660	.000	-.024	.294

quality factor alone does not constitute a quality childcare program (Epstein & Barnett, 2012; Pianta, Downer, & Hamre, 2016). Therefore, high-quality childcare centers were determined via an aggregate of environmental quality (ECERS-R) and whether the childcare center possessed the minimum standard determined in the literature. Analyses in the current literature supported previous literature that childcare centers significantly differ in quality across indicators of quality, including environmental quality, teacher-child interaction, and teacher characteristics. In particular, public prekindergarten programs were rated the highest ratings of ECERS-R scores and the Arnett scores, and teachers on average possessed a graduate degree. However, public prekindergarten programs were not the strongest predictors of prosocial skills, problematic behaviors, or academic-related skills.

Notably, attendance at Head Start programs predicted fewer problematic behaviors. Teachers in Head Starts overall had

Table 5:
Coefficients for Final Model for Predicting Academic-Related Skills

	B	β	t	p	Bivariate r	Partial
Public	.438	.029	3.446	.001	-.044	.035
Private	-.239	-.097	-6.250	.000	.169	-.063
Head Start	.965	.556	14.914	.000	-.245	.148
Preschool/ nursery	1.718	.756	26.388	.000	.244	.256
Other	-.179	-.018	-1.797	.072	.034	-.018
ECERS- inadequate	2.742	1.411	35.748	.000	.074	.338
ECERS-minimal	.906	.437	27.411	.000	-.044	.265
Arnett	.144	1.280	79.897	.000	.224	.626
Education level	-.378	-.712	-36.986	.000	-.099	-.348
Years worked	-.069	-.097	-4.700	.000	-.189	-.047
Diagnosis	.064	.035	2.105	.035	-.146	.021

significantly more years of experience in the workplace than other programs. Private schools predicted better academic-related skills readiness. However, these programs on average were rated as approaching 'minimal' environmental quality as rated by the ECERS-R and had the least experienced teachers of all the childcare programs. One possible explanation for this finding is the vastly different programs that could be considered a "private" program. Given that the childcare types were labeled by the childcare directors themselves, private programs may possibly differ in quality and population served more so than other programs included in the study. In contrast, Head Start is a federally funded program with specific regulations regarding the minimum requirements required for quality. For this reason, Head Start centers are often considered to be "high" on standards for center-based care. Similarly, because public prekindergarten programs are typically offered as an intervention through special education services for children with a disability or children at risk for academic or behavioral delays, they too have specified standards. Whereas Head Start and public preschool programs have regulated quality standards, private programs, child care, and nursery programs all operate under state mandated conditions where there are varying degrees of quality, accreditation, and fee structures. These factors may possibly account for some of the current results.

To determine whether quality childcare programs have a differential affect for children with an independently diagnosed DBD, additional analyses would have to be conducted. However, it is still important to note that children enrolled in quality programs predict higher social-emotional functioning. Teacher-child interaction quality, in particular, was one indicator that significantly predicted prosocial development and has also been shown in the literature to be an important variable in relation to prosocial skills. Teacher-child interactions are useful in modeling appropriate social skills, demonstrating appropriate conflict resolution and coping strategies, and providing positive interactions that are known to decrease problem behaviors in the classroom. For children with disruptive behavior disorders symptoms, positive teacher-child interactions are often recommended for prevention and intervention practices to develop social-emotional skills. As children with DBD symptoms can be challenging, having teachers who are emotionally supportive with strong classroom management skills may be more important than possessing a certain degree or certain years of experience. Positive, individual interactions between teachers and children play a substantial role in school readiness for young children, and it influences education beyond the preschool years. Given the importance of this relationship, Pianta, Barnett, Burchinal, & Thornburg (2009) call for improving teacher-child interaction through professional development activities, including targeted interventions, mentoring, and early childhood training.

Teacher-child interaction was most predictive of prosocial skills and fewer problem behaviors in kindergarten regardless of diagnosis. In terms of school readiness skills, teacher experience and education were most related to academic-related skills. These findings are consistent with studies showing the importance of teacher-child relationships in increasing social-emotional skills (Burchinal et al., 2010; Peisner-Feinberg et al., 2001), while teacher qualifications including years of experience, credentials, and education levels have been shown to increase reading and math skills (Early et al., 2006). Teacher-child interactions were useful in demonstrating appropriate social skills, conflict resolution and coping strategies, and positive interactions.

Limitations of the Study

The current study aimed to understand whether the social-emotional development of children showing DBD symptoms was influenced by the type of childcare attended and how centers scored on indicators of quality. In addition, to determine whether children with DBD symptoms improved in social-emotional development from prekindergarten to kindergarten, a growth analysis would be the most appropriate analysis to conduct to answer these research questions. However, few children within the dataset were identified with DBD symptoms, and even fewer of these children participated in a classroom observation, which provided data regarding the quality of their childcare settings. This led to a small sample size in which the statistical analyses most appropriate to investigate the research question was unable to be completed. While other methods of data analysis were considered (i.e., hierarchical linear modeling), multiple regression was conducted to address the restrictions of the data collected.

Implications for Children from Disadvantaged Backgrounds

Children from disadvantaged backgrounds may face several risk factors associated with school readiness. When children face these risk factors as well as behavioral concerns, children face a disadvantage and do not achieve school readiness to the same level as their peers. Though the current study does not explicitly examine the consequences for children from disadvantaged backgrounds, important inferences can be drawn from the results of the current study. Research suggests positive benefits of attending quality center-based childcare for children living in poverty. There is evidence to suggest that attendance at high-quality preschools have provided cognitive, academic, and social gains for children living in poverty which in turn helped children enter school prepared to succeed. The current study focused on the influence of quality childcare on the social-emotional development of children who demonstrated symptoms of DBD. Results of the study consistently suggested that the teacher-child interaction was significantly related to social-emotional outcomes in school entry regardless of poverty status. Therefore, the quality of the preschool setting was of utmost importance in providing academic, behavioral, and social benefits for children (Burchinal et al., 2002; Burchinal et al., 2010; Peisner-Feinberg et al., 2001; Votruba-Drzal et al., 2004). Quality early childhood education gave young children the opportunity to begin school with the necessary tools to succeed in elementary school and beyond.

Author's Note:

Correspondence concerning this article should be addressed to Sierra Brown, Department of Psychiatry, Penn State Hershey Medical Center, Hershey, PA 17033 Contact: sbrown12@penn-statehealth.psu.edu.

References

Arnett, J. (1989). Caregivers in day-care centers: Does training matter? *Journal of Applied Developmental Psychology, 10*, 541 – 552. doi: 10.1016/0193-3973(89)90026-9

Burchinal, M. R., Cryer, D., Clifford, R. M., & Howes, C. (2002). Caregiver training and classroom quality in child care centers. *Applied Developmental Science, 6*, 2 – 11. doi: 10.1207/S1532480XADS0601_01

Burchinal, M.R., Vandergrift, N., Pianta, R., & Mashburn, A. (2010). Threshold analysis of association between child care quality and child outcomes for low-income children in pre-kindergarten programs. *Early Childhood Research Quarterly, 25,* 166 – 176. doi:10.1016/j.ecresq.2009.10.004

Campbell, F. A., & Pungello E. P. (2007). The Abecedarian Project. In C. Reynolds & E. Fletcher-Janzen (Eds.), *Encyclopedia of special education: A reference for the education of children, adolescents, and adults with disabilities and other exceptional individuals.* Retrieved from http://literati.credoreference.com/content/entry/wileyse/the_abecedarian_project/0

Campbell, S. B. (1994). Hard-to-manage preschool boys: Externalizing behavior, social competence, and family context at a two-year follow up. *Journal of Abnormal Child Psychology, 22,* 147 – 166. doi: 10.1007/BF02167897

DuPaul, G. J., McGoey, K. E., Eckert, T. L., & VanBrakle, J. (2001). Preschool children with attention-deficit/hyperactivity disorder: Impairments in behavioral, social, and school functioning. *Journal of the American Academy of Child and Adolescent Psychiatry, 40,* 508 – 515. doi: 10.1097/00004583-200105000-00009

Early, D. M., Bryant, D. M., Pianta, R. C., Clifford, R. M., Burchinal, M. R., Ritchie, S., ... & Barbarin, O. (2006). Are teachers' education, major, and credentials related to classroom quality and children's academic gains in pre-kindergarten? *Early Childhood Research Quarterly, 21*(2), 174-195. doi:10.1016/j.ecresq.2006.04.004

Economic Policy Institute. (2015, October). *High quality child care is out of reach for working families.* (Issue Brief No. 404). Chicago, IL: Author.

Epstein, D. J., & Barnett, W. S. (2012). Early education in the United States. In R. C. Pianta. (Ed.), *Handbook of early childhood education* (pp. 1 – 21). New York, NY: The Guilford Press.

Gilliam, W. S., & Shahar, G. (2006). Preschool and child care expulsion and suspension: Rates and predictors in one state. *Infants & Young Children, 19,* 228-245.

Graves Jr., S. L., & Howes, C. (2011). Ethnic differences in social-emotional development in preschool: The impact of teacher child relationships and classroom quality. *School Psychology Quarterly, 26,* 202 – 214. doi: 10.1037/a0024117

Gresham, F. M., & Elliott, S. N. (1990). *Social Skills Rating System (SSRS).* Circle Pines, MN: American Guidance Service.

Harms, T., Clifford, R., & Cryer, D. (1998). *Early childhood environment rating scale* (Rev. ed.). New York, NY: Teachers College Press.

Heckman, J. J., Moon, S. H., Pinto, R., Savelyev, P. A., & Yavitz, A. (2010). The rate of return to the High/Scope Perry Preschool Program. *Journal of Public Education, 92*, 114 – 128. doi: 10.3386/w15471

Keys, T. D., Farkas, G., Burchinal, M. R., Duncan, G. J., Vandell, D. L., Weilin, L., …& Howes, C. (2013). Preschool center quality and school readiness: Quality effects and variation by demographic and child characteristics. *Child Development,* doi:10.1111/cdev.12048

Li, W., Farkas, G., Duncan, G. J., Burchinal, M. R., & Vandell, D. L. (2013). Timing of high-quality child care and cognitive, language, and preacademic development. *Developmental Psychology, 49*(8), 1440. doi: 10.1037/a0030613

Loeb, S., Fuller, B., Kagan, S. L., & Carrol, B. (2004). Child care in poor communities: Early learning effects of type, quality, and stability. *Child Development, 75*(1), 47-65.

Magnuson, K. A., Ruhm, C., & Waldfogel, J. (2007). Does prekindergarten improve school preparation and performance? *Economics of Education Review, 26,* 33 – 51. doi:10.1016/j.econedurev.2005.09.008

Mashburn, A. J., Pianta, R. C., Hamre, B. K., Downer, J. T., Barbarin, O. A., Bryant, D., … & Howes, C. (2008). Measures of classroom quality in prekindergarten and children's development of academic, language, and social skills. *Child Development, 79*(3), 732-749.

McCartney, K., Burchinal, M., Clarke-Stewart, A., Bub, K. L., Owen, M. T., Belsky, J., NICHD Early Child Care Research Network. (2010). Testing a series of causal propositions relating time in child care to children's externalizing behavior. *Developmental Psychology, 46*(1), 1 – 17. doi:10.1037/a0017886

Mehaffie, K. E., & Fraser, J. (2007). School readiness: Definitions, best practices, assessments, and cost. In C. J. Groark, K. E. Mehaffie, R. B. McCall, & M. T. Greenberg (Eds.), *Evidence-based practices and programs for early childhood care and education* (pp. 3 – 24). Thousand Oaks, CA: Corwin Press.

Merrell, K. W. (2003). *Preschool and Kindergarten Behavior Scales - Second Edition.* Austin, TX: PRO-ED.

National Institute of Child Health and Human Development (NICHD) Early Child Care Research Network. (2005). Nonmaternal care and family factors in early development: An overview of the NICHD study of early child care. In NICHD Early Child Care Research Network (Ed.), *Child Care and Child Development* (pp. 3 – 38). New York, NY: The Guilford Press.

NICHD Early Child Care Research Network. (2002). Child-care structure→ process→ outcome: Direct and indirect effects of child-care quality on young children's development. *Psychological Science. 13*(3), 199 – 206.

Nix, R. L., Bierman, K. L., Domitrovich, C. E., & Gill, S. (2013). Promoting children's social-emotional skills in preschool can enhance academic and behavioral functioning in kindergarten: Findings from Head Start REDI. *Early Education & Development, 24*(7), 1000-1019. doi: 10.1080/10409289.2013.825565

No Child Left Behind (NCLB) Act of 2001, Pub. L. No. 107-110, § 115, Stat. 1425 (2002).

Peisner-Feinberg, E. S., Burchinal, M. R., Clifford, R. M., Culkin, M. L., Howes, C., Kagan, S. L., & Yazejian, N. (2001). The relation of preschool child-care quality to children's cognitive and social developmental trajectories through second grade. *Child Development, 72*, 1534 – 1553. doi: 10.1111/1467-8624.00364

Pianta, R. C., Barnett, W. S., Burchinal, M., & Thornburg, K. R. (2009). The effects of preschool education what we know, how public policy is or is not aligned with the evidence base, and what we need to know. *Psychological Science in the Public Interest, 10*(2), 49-88. doi: 10.1177/1529100610381908

Pianta, R., Downer, J., & Hamre, B. (2016). Quality in early education classrooms: Definitions, gaps, and systems. *The Future of Children, 26*(2), 119-137.

Piotrkowski, C. S., Botsko, M., & Matthews, E. (2001). Parents' and teachers' beliefs about children's school readiness in a high-need community. *Early Childhood Research Quarterly,* 15, 537-558. doi:10.1016/S0885-2006(01)00072-2

Raver, C. C., & Knitzer, J. (2002). *Ready to enter: What research tells policymakers about strategies to promote social and emotional school readiness among three- and four-year-olds.* New York: National Center for Children in Poverty.

Rose, E. (2010). *The promise of preschool: From Head Start to universal pre-kindergarten.* Oxford, NY: Oxford University Press.

Ryan, R. M., Johnson, A., Rigby, E., & Brooks-Gunn, J. (2011). The impact of child care subsidy use on child care quality. *Early Childhood Research Quarterly, 26*(3), 320-331.

Schweinhart, L. J., Barnes, H. V., & Weikart, D. P. (1993). *Significant benefits: The High/Scope Perry Preschool Study through age 27.* Ypsilanti, MI: The High/Scope Press.

Schweinhart, L. J., Montie, J., Xiang, Z., Barnett, W. S., Belfield, C. R., & Nores, M. (2005). *Lifetime Effects: The High/Scope Perry Preschool Study through age 40.* Ypsilanti, MI: The High/Scope Press.

Schweinhart, L. J., & Weikart, D. P. (1981). Effects of the Perry Preschool Program in youths through age 15. *Journal of Early Intervention, 4*, 29 – 39. doi: 10.1177/105381518100400105

U.S. Department of Health and Human Services. (2010). *Head Start impact study. Final report.* Retrieved from http://www.acf.hhs.gov/sites/default/files/opre/executive_summary_final.pdf

Vandell, D. L., Belsky, J., Burchinal, M., Steinberg, L., Vandergrift, N., & NICHD Early Child Care Research Network. (2010). Do effects of early child care extend to age 15 years? Results from the NICHD study of early child care and youth development. *Child Development, 81*(3), 737-756. doi:10.1111/j.1467-8624.2010.01431.x

Votruba-Drzal, E., Coley, R. L., & Chase-Lansdale, P. L. (2004). Child care and low-income children's development: Direct and moderated effects. *Child Development, 75,* 296-312. doi: 10.1111/j.1467-8624.2004.00670.x

Weikart, D. P., Deloria, D. J., Lawser, S. A., & Wiegerink, R. (1970). *Longitudinal Results of the Perry Preschool Project.* Ypsilanti, MI: High/Scope Educational Research Foundation.

Welsh, J. A., Nix, R. L., Blair, C., Bierman, K. L., & Nelson, K. E. (2010). The development of cognitive skills and gains in academic school readiness for children from low-income families. *Journal of Educational Psychology, 102,* 43 – 53. doi:10.1037/a0016738

Zigler, E., & Styfco, S. J. (2003). The federal commitment to preschool education: Lessons from and for Head Start. In A. J. Reynolds, M. C. Wang, & H. J. Walberg (Eds.), *Early childhood programs for a new century* (pp. 3 – 33). Washington, DC: CWLA Press.

Healthy Infants: Fostering Responsive Caregiving via Tiered Mentoring for High-Risk Teen Mothers and Infants

Tracy K. Larson, Stephen J. Bagnato, Maura A. Miglioretti, Carol Barone-Martin, and Robin McNeal

Abstract

Research implications of cumulative poverty, adverse childhood events, and toxic stress on the development and overall future health of young children and families make clear that promotion and prevention programs are necessary. Early Head Start (EHS) is the seminal prevention program for high-risk infants/toddlers and parents. This pilot study explored the elements and impacts of the *Healthy Infants* (HI) promotion and prevention tiered mentoring model of face-to-face and virtual strategies for infant-parent-teacher triads. The HI model strives to promote the acquisition of protective developmental competencies for resiliency and the precursors for early school success, and to prevent and disrupt the early cumulative developmental effects of adverse childhood events (ACEs) and toxic stress in the lives of high-risk infants/toddlers and parents by targeting: a) responsive parenting, b) caregiving competencies, and c) use of best practices by EHS teachers. Overall, the HI promotion and prevention mentoring model was associated with statistically significant increases in responsive parenting and other caregiving competencies (e.g., affection, encouragement, and teaching). Additional positive outcomes were obtained and are discussed.

Key Words: high-risk, infants, parents, mentoring, promotion, prevention

Numerous research studies highlight the insidious negative impact of cumulative ACEs and associated "toxic stress," particularly the effects of poverty, on overall child development, school success, adult physical health, and successful adaptation in life (Blair & Raver, 2012; Shonkoff, Richter, Vander Gaag, & Bhutta, 2012; Yoshikawa, Aber, & Beardslee, 2012). These cumulative ACEs include: lack of emotional attachments to caregiver; changes in caregivers; recurrent family crisis incidents; homelessness; hunger and malnutrition; physical, sexual, and emotional abuse; divorce and/or domestic violence; chronic unemployment; single-teen-parent head of household; lack of parental education; poor role models for temperament and self-regulatory behavior; illness or chronic medical conditions in family members; drug/alcohol abuse; community violence; and parent incarceration. The more chronic and recurrent the adverse events in a child's life, the higher the risk for "toxic stress" and future neurodevelopmental, behavioral, learning, and chronic medical problems (Felitti, Anda, & Nordenberf, 1998).

Risk Profiles for Teen Mothers and Infants

Teen parents are a unique risk factor for infants/toddlers. Teen parents are often single parents with limited resources. They often have fewer protective factors such as supportive adult relationships and role models (McDonald et al., 2009). Young parents can lack maturity and parenting skills, and typically have greater economic disadvantages (Smith, Gilmer, Salge, Dickerson, & Wilson, 2013). Many teen parents have unrealistic expectations of their children's development, and are less responsive in their interactions with their infants (Holub et al., 2007). Children of teenage parents are at higher risk of showing social-emotional and behavioral disorders, cognitive delays, and lower educational attainment (Holub et al., 2007; McDonald et al., 2009). As these children grow older, they continue to exhibit disparities, compared to same-age peers, in cognitive, behavioral, and health outcomes. Throughout elementary school and into adolescence, teen parents' children continue to fall farther behind their same-aged peers (Mollborn, Lawrence, James-Hawkins, & Fomby, 2014).

The Promise of Tiered Intervention Approaches: Impact on Risk and Resiliency

The risks infants of teen parents face underscore the need to identify and provide appropriate intervention and programmatic support (Holub et al., 2007). Recognizing interventions with teenage parents and their infants/toddlers can play a vital role in preventing negative cycles, and there has been a call to expand the number of services to this group (Mayers, Hager-Budny, & Buckner, 2008). Acknowledging early childhood as an ideal time for interventions that will then improve later life conditions for infants and families, researchers and policymakers have responded with guidance on focusing in the early developmental period (Mollborn et al., 2014).

Recommendations from the National Research Council and the Institute on Medicine [NRCIM], (2000) advocate for designing graduated prevention-oriented programs and individualized interventions to promote caregiving and child development so as to blunt the impact of adverse events and toxic stress in addition to the effects of poverty and lack of positive opportunities in high-risk children and families. Prevention science studies emphasize the ameliorative effect of these models when the focus is on providing nurturing experiences to increase resiliency and coping skills for young children and families (Biglan, Flay, Empty, & Sandler, 2012; Shonkoff & Garner, 2011).

The use of tiered models of promotion and prevention supports are known as Response-to-Intervention (RTI) models and are justified by federal regulations in the IDEA amendments (Office of Special Education Programs [OSEP], 2010). Although most studies on tiered promotion and prevention models have been conducted on school-age students, researchers have begun to validate such tiered models for preschool children (Lehman, Salaway, Bagnato, Grom, & Willard, 2010). To capitalize on the success of the school aged RTI process, and make needed accommodations for younger children, there have been several field validation studies. For example, the *Pyramid*

Model, where supports are provided at different levels of intensity ranging from classroom-wide to individual support was conducted by Hemmeter, Snyder, Fox, and Algina (2016), and Lehman et al., (2010). Bagnato, Salaway, and Suen (2009), and later, Gilliam, Maupin, and Reyes (2016) considered the role of improving teacher skills. Crusto et al. (2013) implemented universal classroom and child-specific strategies and added parent support and education, and home-based intensive interventions. Ocasio, Alst, Koivunen, Huang, and Allegra, (2015) considered the effect of a sequenced curriculum to address listening, focusing attention, self-talk, assertiveness, empathy, emotional management, friendship skills, and problem solving to all children in the classrooms. These authors also embed mental health clinicians in the classrooms, and provide play therapy for children in need of individualized services.

Not surprisingly, pyramid models for young children (age 3-5 years) incorporate several of the key elements identified in research by the NRCIM (2011), and align with developmentally-appropriate practices for effective prevention and promotion. Many of these studies also indicate the elements of the prevention and promotion model elements or tiers that have been shown to increase resiliency and coping skills for young children and families (Biglan et al., 2012; Shonkoff & Garner, 2011). The following list summarizes some of the elements which have shown protective and positive neurodevelopmental effects: longer program participation, responsive caregiver-child attachments, parent engagement, direct child teaching and interventions, emphasis on social-emotional and early literacy competencies, individualization, high program quality, standards-driven best professional practices mentored and modeled for teachers and parents, community-based leadership driving innovative interagency supports, public/private partnerships, and preschool-school linkages (Ramey & Ramey, 1998; Shonkoff et al., 2012).

Findings from these studies demonstrate that early childhood intervention programs and support in natural community settings, which encompass specific programmatic features and elements, can have substantial benefits for young children and families. Adding to this positive literature on prevention programs, Bagnato, Suen, Brantley, Smith-Jones, & Dettore, (2002) conducted ground-breaking longitudinal studies across Pennsylvania for over 15,000 high-risk preschool children (0-6 years of age) in high-poverty and high ACE risk in rural and urban school district-community partnerships to demonstrate the positive developmental and behavioral impact and parent engagement for high quality preschool programs (Bagnato et al., 2009).

Taken altogether, it is clear that in the era of public health initiatives, interagency and interdisciplinary supports involving physical and behavioral health, and family support must be integrated into traditional EHS programs in order to promote the coping, resiliency, and progress of the most vulnerable families. Likewise, the integration of tiered supports in EHS programs can strengthen the competencies of parents and teachers. To date, although tiered models have been implemented and proven effective for children age three to school-age, no tiered promotion and prevention model synthesizes the most efficacious elements from prior studies for application to high-risk infants/toddlers, parents, and EHS teachers.

Purpose of this Pilot Study

The purpose of this pilot study was to explore the elements and impact of the HI promotion and prevention mentoring model for high-risk infants/toddlers, parents, and EHS teachers in the metropolitan city of Pittsburgh, Pennsylvania. The essential objective of this study was to determine if the HI model is associated with the enhancement of responsive parenting and caregiving competencies by parents with their infants/toddlers, and the increased use of best practices by EHS teachers. The central questions of this program evaluation research were:

• Did high-risk parents who received HI model supports over an 8-month period demonstrate a significant enhancement in their responsive parenting and caregiving competencies (e.g., affection, encouragement, and teaching)?

• Did high-risk infants/toddlers of parents who received HI model supports demonstrate reductions in the scope of their atypical development (e.g., improved social and self-regulatory behaviors and decreases in extremes of temperament?

• Did EHS teachers who received HI model supports demonstrate an increase in their use of best practices (e.g., nurturing and responsive relationships, supportive environments, targeted social emotional strategies, and individualized interventions) and in the quality of their classroom's climate (e.g. developmentally-appropriate practices)?

Methods

This study was conducted in the metropolitan area of Pittsburgh, Pennsylvania. Several urban areas have been affected by chronic socio-economic distress and poverty, poor nutrition, unsafe housing, inadequate drinking water, and limited medical resources, as well as high unemployment, inadequate infrastructure, and lack of social service and health care opportunities which impact the health of this population (Healthy People, 2010). The percentage of children in poverty ranges from 23% to 38%, another 19.7% are in families between 100% and 199% of the federal poverty level, and 18.3% have special health care needs as compared to a national rate of 13.9%, (Centers for Disease Control [CDC], 2008); ACE score risk levels exceed four, placing individuals for negative health and mental health outcomes across their lifetime.

Participants

Participants (infants/toddlers, parents, and teachers) were recruited from an EHS program. At the time of this data collection, 48 infants/toddlers had parents and teachers participating in tiers 1-3 of the HI model whereas 21 had completed all five tiers of the pyramid model. Of the 21 completed, two parents withdrew and two aged-out of the EHS program, leaving a total of 17 parents. Ultimately, 13 of the participating parents provided various pieces of information for analysis; one parent had two infant/toddlers participating. Demographic information was collected on all infants/toddlers, parents, and teachers. Outcome measures were collected only on parents, infants/toddlers, and teachers receiving services in tiers four or five.

Parent participants. Table 1 provides an overview of parent data, including where information was omitted. For this reason, the number of participants in each parent level analysis below varies. Table 2 describes parent demographic information ($n = 10$).

Infant/toddlers. Table 3 provides data on infants/toddlers.

Teacher participants. Eight teachers (lead and assistants) from four EHS classrooms, participated in the HI model. One classroom was located in an Early Childhood Center and three classrooms were located in high schools. The EHS coordinator, family support specialist, education coach, early interventionists, and related service providers were also often participants; however, they were not part of the outcome analysis. See Table 4 for teacher demographic information.

HI Model Implementation

Implementation team. Five trained specialists (early interventionist, developmental school psychologist, developmental healthcare consultants, and a consulting pediatric nurse practitioner) acted as mentors to the teachers delivering the intervention in this study. HI mentors were masters or doctoral-level staff working

Table 1:
Number of Participants Responding to Each Outcome Measure

Measure	Responded	Omitted
Parent demographic information	10	3
Child demographic information	11	3
Caregiver ACES	9	4
Child ACES	11	3
PICCOLO	12	2
TABS	7	7

Note: PICCOLO = Parenting Interactions with Children: Checklist of Observations Linked to Outcomes; TABS = The Temperament and Atypical Behavior Scale.

Table 2:
Parent and Family Demographic Characteristics

Characteristic	N	Characteristic	N
Age		**Number of children**	
19 or younger	7	1	7
20 or older	3	2	2
Sex		3	1
Female	9	**Housing**	
Male	1	Rent	3
Ethnicity		Share	5
African American	7	Transitional	2
Biracial	1	**Disability***	
Caucasian	1	Disabled	3
Hispanic	1	Non-Disabled	6
Marital Status		**Social serviced involvement**	
Single	9	Current	4
Married	1	Past	1
		Never	5

*Note: One parent omitted this item

Table 3:
Child (Total N = 11) Demographic Characteristics

Characteristic	N
Birth year	
2014	4
2013	1
2012	3
2011	3
Sex	
Female	4
Male	7
Ethnicity	
African American	8
Biracial	3

Table 4:
Teacher (N = 6) Demographic Information

Title	N
Lead teacher	3
Teaching assistant	3
Sex	
Female	6
Male	0
Ethnicity	
Caucasian	3
African American	3
Teaching Experience (in years)	
5 or less	2
5-10	2
10 or more	2
Degree Level	
Bachelor's Degree	6

at the University of Pittsburgh Office of Child Development, or student interns completing a master's degree in psychology, special education, or social work.

Implementation process. HI mentors were trained to have knowledge in infant and toddler development, adult learning, collaborative consultation and problem solving, mentoring, motivational interviewing, evidence-based observation and promotion-prevention-intervention strategies, and HI model elements, processes, and procedures. In addition to the mentoring role, specialists were also trained as teacher, parent, and child assessors with structured observational tools (The Pyramid Infant-Toddler Observation Scale [TPITOS], Parenting Interactions with Children Checklist of Observations Linked to Outocmes [PICCOLO]), rating scales (Temperament and Atypical Behavior Scale [TABS]), and surveys (demographic and ACES).

At the start of the study, HI mentors introduced the HI model, goals, benefits, and responsibilities in participation and overall processes to parents and EHS teachers. HI mentoring was provided equally to a lead teacher and an assistant teacher. The HI team also met weekly to share professional knowledge and provide interdisciplinary perspectives.

Previous federal research on teacher mentoring in Head Start (Bagnato, Seo, Salaway, & Kim, 2016) demonstrated that mentoring of seven hours per week (28 hours per month) resulted in significant improvements in a teacher's use of best practice as indicated on the norm-referenced observational measures. HI mentors provided seven hours per week of face-to-face and virtual mentoring to teachers and parents in delivering the HI model. HI mentors implemented the following five HI model elements, which have been identified as promising effective elements in other studies, with the participants for 1-2 years depending on their point of entry.

Element 1: Tiered promotion and prevention services and supports. The HI model incorporated the foundational features of the field-validated *Teaching Pyramid from the Center for Social-*

Emotional Foundations of Early Learning (CSEFEL; Fox, Carta, Strain, Dunlap, & Hemmeter, 2010) as a framework for implementing the remaining four elements. CSEFEL's Pyramid model includes 1) effective workforce, 2) nurturing and responsive relationships, 3) high quality supportive environments, 4) targeted social emotional supports, and 5) intensive interventions. These components served as the foundation and organizing framework for HI's tiered promotion and prevention services and supports. Table 5 illustrates the HI model elements implemented across tiers.

Element 2: Transagency teamwork. HI mentors worked in partnership with EHS program's education coaches, family support specialists, and supervisors to mentor parent-infant-teacher triads via a mobile transagency interdisciplinary team. The transagency team had representatives from the HI team (generalists and specialists including a masters-level developmental healthcare consultant, an applied developmental psychologist, and a consulting pediatric nurse practitioner), and the EHS program (e.g., education coach, family support specialist, education supervisor). The HI mentor offered the specific mentoring, developmental/behavioral health consultation, and promotion-prevention-intervention strategies that enabled teachers to build their use of best practice and responsive caregiving competencies, and improve the overall climate of their EHS classroom. The education supervisor represented the organizational commitment for linking HI mentoring with supervisory and programmatic support to teachers within EHS regulations. The transagency team worked together to support infants/toddlers, parents, and each other while addressing individual, group, and program needs.

Element 3: Curriculum-guided responsive caregiving. HI tiered mentoring focused upon the 29 critical parenting competencies of the PICCOLO (Roggman, Cook, Innocenti, Jump, & Christiansen, 2013) which best predict positive infant-parent outcomes have been field-validated in the EHS Family and Child Experiences Survey (FACES; Xue et al., 2014), in developmental research during standardization

(Cook & Roggman, 2009), and supported by the NRCIM (2000) *Neurons to Neighborhoods* report on the importance of responsive caregiving relationships and social-emotional competencies. HI mentors nurtured relationships between parent-infant-teacher triads using such varied strategies as face-face modeling, parent group peer-mentoring and cell-phone and iPad video feedback. The HI mentor structures the mentoring process to focus on critical and measurable changes in relationships and the use of "best practices" with high-risk infants/toddlers and families. HI mentors focused on individual, small group, and peer mentoring of parents and EHS teachers during developmental activities and teaching routines in the natural center environment following the mentoring methodology from previous field-validation research (Bagnato et al., 2016).

Element 4: Mobile technology & telemedicine consultation. Capitalizing on the integral use of text-messaging among teenagers and young adults, HI mentors utilized text messages as another support mechanism in disseminating information and supporting young parents both within and outside of the face-to-face mentoring sessions. Text-messaging between the HI mentor and parent or EHS teacher is critical for immediate reinforcement of mentored practices. HI mentors used snap videos focusing upon "positive" parent-infant-teacher interactions to support and supplement face-to-face mentoring. The videos highlighted responsive interactions and provided powerful visual images of status and change in caregiving during mentoring.

Distance technology is also important to engage interdisciplinary partners on the team and provided a vehicle and opportunity for formal and episodic consultation between other professionals such as early intervention specialists, health specialists, and human service representatives. HI mentors utilized the Health Insurance Portability and Accountability Act (HIPPA)-compliant software to provide tele-medicine consultation from a certified pediatric nurse practitioner and psychologist and Skype and FaceTime were used to enable HI mentors to answer EHS teacher questions about particular individual infant/toddler or parent needs as well as to conduct short tutorials on critical professional development topics such as nutrition, relationships with primary care physicians, medical conditions, management of atypical self-regulatory behaviors, and identifying risk and delay.

Element 5: University-community partnerships for interdisciplinary education. HI mentors provided training to EHS teachers who received professional development and continuing education credits for their engagement in various HI promotion and prevention supports: face-face and virtual mentoring, formal workshops, webinars, and telemedicine consultation. University mentors provided participants with education and training which aligned with Pennsylvania state-documented Pennsylvania Quality Assurance System (PQAS) and Act 48 education credits.

Measures

PICCOLO. *The PICCOLO* (Roggman et al., 2013) is a norm-referenced checklist of 29 observable developmentally supportive parenting behaviors, which is field-validated nationally for the use of assessing and planning for goals to promote responsive parenting (Bagnato, Neisworth, & Pretti-Frontczak, 2010; Xue et al., 2014). The PICCOLO includes measures of parental affection (e.g., "parent speaks in a warm tone of voice"), parental responsiveness (e.g. "parent responds to child's emotions"), parental encouragement (e.g., "parent supports child in making choices"), and teaching interactions (e.g., "parent engages in pretend play with child"). Together, these factors are thought to contribute to positive parent-child relationships.

TABS. *The TABS* Screener is a norm-referenced, nationally standardized, 15-item rating scale designed to identify temperament and self-regulation problems that can indicate that a child is developing atypically or is at risk for atypical development (Bagnato, Neisworth, & Salvia, 1999; Neisworth,

Bagnato, & Hunt, 1999). The TABS is commonly used for early screening and intervention programs in the United States and is one of only four instruments recommended for use with infants and young children by the American Academy of Pediatrics (AAP; Bagnato et al., 1999). A TABS rating of 1-2 indicates a strong risk for atypical development. A rating of three or more indicates a 95% chance that the infant/toddler will demonstrate temperament and self-regulation problems on the full 55-item TABS.

TPITOS. TPITOS is an assessment instrument designed to measure the fidelity of implementation of practices associated with the Pyramid Model in infant/toddler care settings (Hemmeter, 2009). The TPITOS provides a classroom snapshot of adult behaviors and classroom environment variables that are associated with supporting and promoting the social-emotional development of infants/toddlers. The TPITOS is completed based on a two-hour observation conducted in infant/toddler classrooms (birth to age three), followed by an interview with the teacher. TPITOS data may be used to support professional development in the following ways: 1) identifying and making explicit the specific competencies that promote social-emotional development; 2) providing team and individual teacher feedback to reinforce teacher strengths; 3) guiding individual and team targeted goal-setting to strengthen teacher competencies; and 4) monitoring growth relevant to professional development competencies.

ACES. *The Adverse Childhood Events Survey* (Felitti et al., 1998) measures three areas of adverse childhood events: abuse, neglect, and household dysfunction. More specifically, the survey asks if the parent or child has been physically, emotionally or sexually abused, physically or emotionally neglected, or if mental health, domestic violence, divorce, incarceration, or substance abuse is present within the household. According to the ACEs study a higher ACE score indicates the higher likelihood of various health problems later in life (Felitti et al., 1998).

Table 5:
Specific HI Elements and Strategies Across Tiers

Tier & % coverage	Elements and common strategies	Teacher-infant	Parent-infant
Tiers 1-3: Professional development mentoring to promote best practices, responsive caregiving and quality classrooms **100% Coverage** Universal-entire program	•On-site and virtual interdisciplinary education and mentoring to enhance use of best practices, quality classrooms and responsive relationships	x	x
	•Interdisciplinary and transagency team-building activities	x	
	•Assessment of "best practices", quality of classroom environment and teacher-parent and teacher-infant interactions	x	
	•Assessment of infant/toddler's social-emotional development	x	x
	•Assessment of family needs and risk factors		x
	•On-site demonstrating and modeling	x	
Tier 4: Mentoring with small groups of parents and teachers on strategies to promote the acquisition of caregiving competencies and positive social-emotional development **50% Coverage** Selected need groups	•On-site and virtual interdisciplinary education and mentoring to enhance targeted social emotional supports	x	x
	•Collaborative development of classroom goals and plans based on assessment	x	
	•On-site demonstrating and modeling to enhance targeted social emotional supports	x	x
Tier 5: Mentoring individual parents and teachers on strategies to prevent developmental disabilities and support the most complex needs. **10-15% Coverage** Individual needs Parent-infant-teacher triads	•On-site and virtual interdisciplinary education and mentoring on individual interventions	x	x
	•Additional assessment of parent-infant-teacher interactions, family strengths & needs, infant's development	x	x
	•Collaborative development of individual parent-infant-teacher plans to enhance responsive caregiving	x	x
	•On-site individual mentoring, demonstrating and modeling of individualized interventions	x	x
	•Use of teacher-infant and parent-infant interaction video for feedback as a behavior change strategy	x	x
	•Interdisciplinary and interagency teaming; linkages to additional services	x	x
	•Individual parent-infant-teacher consultation from pediatric nurse practitioner or psychologist	x	x

Research Design

HI utilized a repeated-measures, pre-test, post-test single group design (Cook & Campbell, 1979) to evaluate the effectiveness of improving parent-child interactions, teacher-child competencies, and reducing child risk for atypical development. Prior to HI program implementation, parents were observed and rated using the PICCOLO to evaluate the quality of mother-infant/toddler interactions. Teachers were observed by trained HI personnel, and their teaching interactions were rated with the TPITOS. Children's behaviors were rated using the TABS screener to evaluate their current risk for atypical development. These measures provided baseline ratings of parent, teacher, and child behavior, and were administered at the completion of the program to evaluate the effects of HI on parent, child, and teacher variables. Individual participants within the study thus acted as their own control.

HI mentors examined the formative results of the above pre-intervention measures to identify the strengths and needs of participants, and to initiate tiered mentoring based on their analysis and observations. Mentoring services extended from September to June of two school years. Mentors and teaching teams or parents collaboratively set individualized goals. During the mentoring process, mentors encouraged teachers' and parents' reflection on their current practices and their experimentation with newly learned techniques. Post-test data were collected on teachers' and parents' practices after mentoring at the end of the study using the TPITOS and PICCOLO.

Results

ACES

Nine caregivers in the program reported on their personal traumatic life experiences using the ACES. According to the Adverse Childhood Experiences Study a higher ACE score indicates the higher likelihood of various health problems later in life (Felitti et al., 1998). Within this cohort, all but one caregiver reported experiencing multiple traumas, with a median of six different types of traumatic experiences reported (min = 1, max = 8). The high-risk cutoff in national research is at 2-3 for later medical and mental health diagnoses. Table 6 shows parent ACES endorsements. Caregivers also reported on the traumatic experiences of their young children ($N = 11$). Within the cohort, all but one child had experienced multiple types of traumatic experiences, with a mean of four different types of experiences reported (min = 1, max = 8).

The high-risk cut-off in national research is at 2-3 for later medical and mental health diagnoses. See Table 7 for infant/toddler ACES endorsements.

HI Outcomes

Infant outcomes. The self-regulatory behaviors of infants/toddlers were evaluated with the TABS screener (Bagnato et al., 1999). On the TABS screener, endorsement of at least two behaviors indicates that the child is at risk for atypical development and self-regulatory behavior. Endorsement of three or more indicates that the infant/toddler's temperament and self-regulatory behaviors are likely atypical for his or her age. Of the seven infants/toddlers who were evaluated, six had a reduction in maladaptive behaviors after participation by the parent in HI. One infant/toddler had a drastic increase (+6) in maladaptive behaviors, and represented a significant outlier in the group. Before HI tiered mentoring, a median of 3.5 maladaptive behaviors were reported, indicating significant signs of atypical temperament and self-regulation. After HI tiered mentoring, maladaptive behaviors were reduced to a median of 0.5, indicating a reduction to minimal risk of atypicality (See Figure 1). Reduction of maladaptive behaviors below the threshold of three indicates that children in the HI program experienced a reduced risk for atypical development.

Parent outcomes. HI used the PICCOLO to record and rate the parent's level of responsive parenting and caregiving behaviors with their infants/toddlers. In total, 13 parents and their infant/toddlers had their interactions observed and rated using the PICCOLO at entry to the program. Only 12 parents-infant dyads were evaluated using the PICCOLO after HI tiered mentoring was completed. One parent-infant pair experienced a large reduction in positive interactions in every domain of the PICCOLO for unknown reasons (See Figure 2). This represented an extreme outlier of the group, and was thus eliminated from analysis leaving a total of 11 repeated measures cases for analysis.

Table 6:
Parent (Total possible N = 9) ACES Endorsements and Tally of ACES experiences

Experience	N
Physical abuse	5
Emotional abuse	7
Sexual abuse	0
Drug and alcohol abuse in home	5
Caregiver incarceration	5
Family mental health concern	9
Domestic violence	3
Absent caregiver	7
Physical neglect	4
Emotional neglect	4

Total Number of Experiences	
1 or less	1
2-5	2
6 or more	6

Table 7:
Infant/toddler (Total possible N = 11) ACES Endorsements and Tally of ACES Experiences

Experience	N
Physical abuse	0
Emotional abuse	2
Sexual abuse	0
Drug and alcohol abuse in home	6
Caregiver incarceration	9
Family mental health concern	8
Domestic violence	3
Absent caregiver	6
Physical neglect	5
Emotional neglect	5

Total Number of Experiences	
1 or less	1
2-5	7
6 or more	3

Due to the use of a repeated measures design, a paired-samples t-test was conducted to analyze the effects of HI on positive parent-infant/toddler interactions as measured by the PICCOLO (Roggman et al., 2013). On average, parents engaged in more positive and responsive interactions with their infants/toddlers after participation in HI tiered mentoring (*M* = 32.09; SD = 8.32) than before (*M* = 20.82; SD = 9.24). This difference, 11.27, 95% Confidence Interval [5.49, 17.06], was significant t (10) = 4.34, p < .005, and represented a moderate effect r = .65 (See Table 8 and Figure 2).

HI tiered mentoring had a significant, small effect on parents responsiveness to their infants/toddlers (Mean difference = 4.18, 95% CI [2.48-5.88], *t* (10) = 5.50, *p* < .001, *r* = .28), a significant, large effect on their encouraging interactions (Mean difference = 2.63, 95% CI [.42-4.85], *t* (10) = 2.65, *p* < .05, *r* = .75, and a significant, large effect on their teaching interactions (Mean difference = 1.91, 95% CI [.77-3.05], *t* (10) = 3.72, *p* < .005, *r* = .58). HI did not have a significant effect on parental affection toward their infants/toddlers, p = .075.

Figure 1:
TABS median scores before and after HI model implementation

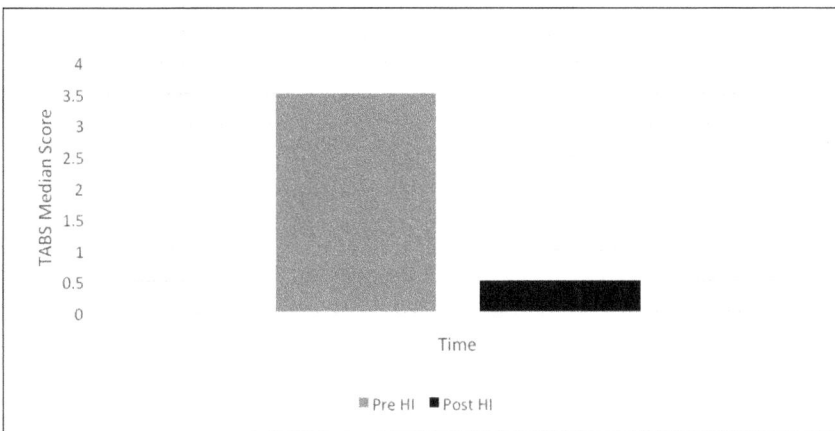

Using descriptive statistics on PICCOLO scores, teen parents (age 19 or younger) demonstrated greater improvement in positive and responsive parent-infant interactions (Mean difference = 11.5) than non-teen parents (Mean difference = 6.7) when comparing pre:post HI group means by caregiver age. This underscores the importance of early intervention for at-risk parent-infant dyads. When comparing pre:post HI group means by parent ACES tally, parents who experienced less than the cohort median of six types of traumatic experiences benefited the most from HI, as per composite PICCOLO scores (Mean difference = 27). Parents with more than six types of traumatic experiences saw less of an improvement in positive parent-infant interactions (Mean difference = 7.5). While only two caregivers who completed the PICCOLO experienced less than six traumatic experiences, the large difference in PICCOLO improvement between groups can still point to the cumulative effects of trauma on parent-infant interactions.

Program/provider outcomes. In order to measure the quality and climate of the classroom's social and physical environment and the competencies of teachers in areas of social emotional development, HI utilized the TPITOS observation scale on three of the four classrooms. The TPITOS evaluates the developmental appropriateness of the EHS classroom climate and physical and social environment, using Likert Scale items with possible scores ranging from 1-4. In total, three EHS classrooms provided an instructional environment to the infants/toddlers enrolled in HI; 55% of the participating children attended school A, 18% were enrolled in school B, and 9% were enrolled in school C. The remaining (18%) of children in the study were in a classroom that was not observed using the TPITOS. In the three participating schools, lead teachers established environments approaching ideal levels of best practice, as indicated by average TPITOS pre-intervention ratings between "emerging" and "exemplary" (M = 3.67; SD = .208) prior to HI tiered mentoring. After HI tiered mentoring,

Table 8:
Pairwise comparison results (PICCOLO T1 vs. PICCOLO T2)

Domain	Mean difference	Std. dev	95% CI	t	Sig. (2-tailed)	Effect size correlation
PICCOLO composite	11.27273	8.61500	5.4859-17.06036	4.340	.001*	.653
Affection	2.54545	4.25120	-.31054-5.40145	1.986	.075	-
Responsiveness	4.18182	2.52262	2.48710-5.87654	5.498	.000*	.282
Encouragement	2.63636	3.29462	.42301-4.84972	2.654	.024*	.751
Teaching	1.90909	1.70027	.77684-3.051	3.724	.004*	.581

Note: Significant results, defined by p < .05, are marked with an asterisk (*). CI = confidence interval; Std. dev = standard deviation.

Figure 2:
PICCOLO median scores before and after HI model implementation

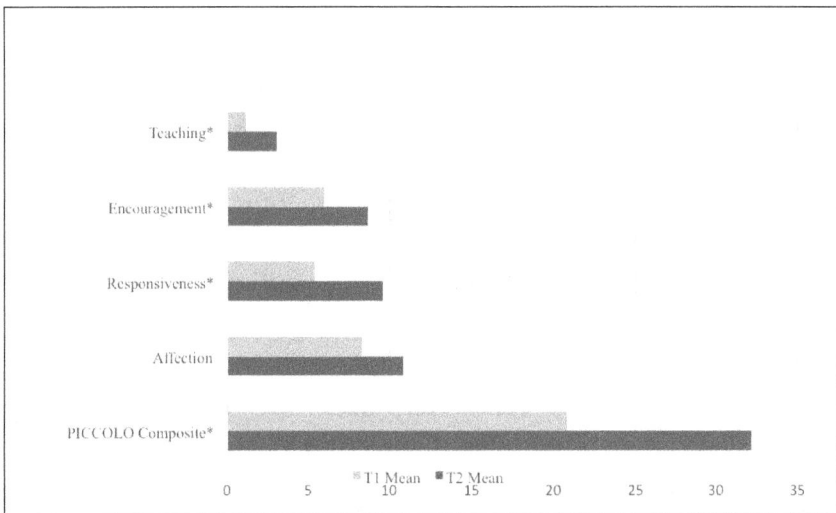

Note: Significant results, defined by p < .05, are marked with an asterisk (*).

teachers on average improved their interactions with children and their classroom environment, as indicated by an increase in the average observational item score on the TPITOS ($M = 3.84$; $SD = .17$). See Figure 3 for average item score for each teacher before and after HI implementation. This equates to an average 4.3-point increase on the overall TPITOS measure, and an overall improvement in the developmental appropriateness of the EHS classroom. Prior to HI tiered mentoring, teachers scored a total score of 88 out of a possible 96 points on the TPITOS (91.6%); This is notable due to the limited room for positive growth created by the maximum score obtainable on the measure. An increase to a total score of 92.3 (96.2%) on the TPITOS, with a reduction in standard deviation, indicates that the quality of the EHS classroom improved and the EHS teachers were able to more closely approach ideal levels of support. This change suggests that HI tiered mentoring helped to create EHS classrooms that were more developmentally-appropriate and supportive, and worked to bring all classrooms to comparable levels of quality.

Discussion

The pilot study investigated the impact of the HI tiered mentoring model on enhancing high-risk parent's responsive parenting and caregiving competencies, reducing atypical self-regulatory behaviors in their high-risk infants/toddlers, and improving overall EHS classroom quality and climate. This is the first pilot study of HI as a tiered mentoring model for promotion and prevention. Overall, the HI tiered mentoring model was associated with statistically significant increases in responsive parenting and caregiving competencies. In addition, high-risk infants/toddlers whose parents were involved in HI showed reductions in atypical behaviors; teachers who received HI mentoring showed improvements in their competencies and the quality of EHS classrooms improved.

Parents in this study engaged in more positive and responsive interactions with their infants/toddlers after participation in HI tiered mentoring. On average, parents showed significant increases in positive and responsive interactions with their children (going from $M = 32.09$ down to $M = 20.82$). While inferential comparisons could not be made due to study limitations, the apparent effect of HI as indicated by mean-difference scores on the PICCOLO paired with a reduction in maladaptive infant/toddler behaviors as measured by the TABS (six of the seven infants/toddlers evaluated showed a reduction in maladaptive behaviors, from a median of 3.5 to a median of .5) indicates that HI tiered mentoring has the likely effect of mitigating risk for atypical development and problematic self-regulatory behaviors in high-risk populations. Prior to HI tiered mentoring, infants/toddlers in the study displayed significant signs of atypical extremes of temperament and self-regulatory behaviors. After HI tiered mentoring, these behaviors were reduced, minimizing the risk of atypical development. Additionally, parents

Figure 3:
Lead teacher TPITOS ratings before and after HI implementation

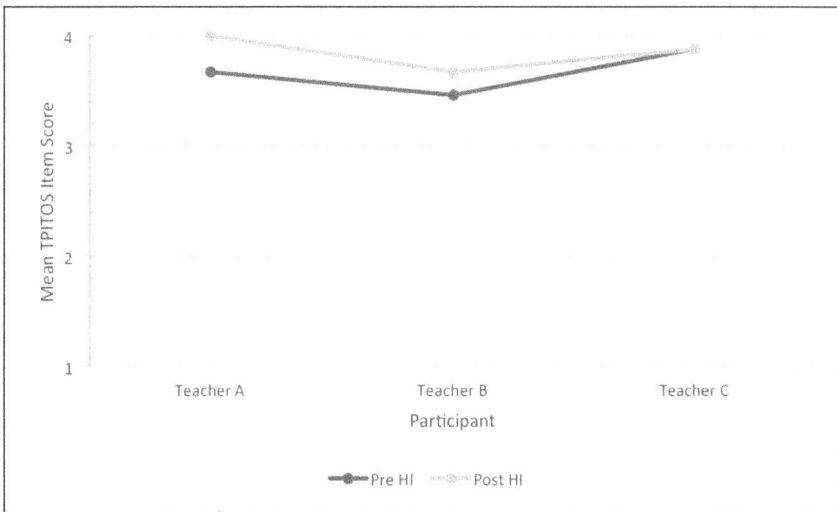

with five or fewer types of adverse experiences benefited the most from HI, while parents with more than five improved less. This is in-line with research about how adverse events and toxic stress hinder a parent's capacity to provide responsive caregiving.

EHS teachers participating in HI tiered mentoring entered the program as already high-quality, highly-trained educators. This is exemplified by the high mean pre-intervention ratings on the TPITOS. These teachers were responsive to HI tiered mentoring and demonstrated improvements in their competencies and classroom quality which began at nearly ideal levels of quality, which are defined by a score of four ($M = 3.67$ increased to $M = 3.84$). Considering the high average scores of teachers before the intervention and the limited room for upward growth, the reduction of the variance between pre and post-test TPITOS scores of the teachers shows that the intervention succeeded in its mission to improve EHS classroom quality. With only three teachers evaluated, inferential comparisons were not possible. However, should HI be replicated and implemented on a larger cohort of teachers, infants/toddlers and parents, it is hypothesized that HI would have a similar positive effect.

Adverse life events clearly put infants/toddlers at high risk for developmental, behavioral, learning, and medical problems. Children living below the federal poverty level experience substantial adverse life events associated with poverty, putting them at high risk for atypical development. All infants/toddlers and their parents fell below the federal poverty level as indicated by their eligibility and enrollment in EHS. As such, these infants/toddlers have accumulated risk for atypical development related to barriers to quality health care, mental health care, and education, and increased risk for exposure to trauma, and effects of other cumulative adverse live events. These adverse experiences were quantified in this study for participants, and were endorsed at levels indicative of a high-risk for future developmental, behavioral, learning, and health problems.

Limitations of the Study

The HI tiered mentoring model was implemented in an EHS program with a high turnover rate for families. The beginning cohort of 22 families was diminished over time, leaving only 10 parent-infant dyads that could be used for analysis. Much of the data gathered on the parents, infants/toddlers represented a particular population; that of impoverished families. As such, many parents reported similar rates of personal trauma experiences leaving little variance in the sample. The skewedness of the data may appear to be a limitation; however, this skew could also typify the population being studied. The cycle of poverty resists regression to the mean. Despite the small sample size, parent interactions as rated on the PICCOLO significantly improved after participation in HI tiered mentoring, and represented a moderate effect. This is promising considering the size of the sample and the strength of the association between HI and the outcome measure. It is hypothesized that if applied to a larger, more heterogeneous sample that the effects would remain and likely show similar associations.

Many participants in the study omitted items in the demographics survey, leaving missing data. There was also a consistent pattern in the data omitted - namely, items that asked about abuse experiences of their infants/toddlers. Many parents also omitted sensitive items for themselves. This is a common difficulty when asking participants about sensitive topics, and is a barrier to correlating parental adverse experiences to child outcomes.

Future Directions

Despite the limitations, the present findings have important initial implications for practice and policy. HI appears to be a promising promotion and prevention mentoring model for enhancing high-risk parent's responsive parenting and caregiving competencies, reducing atypical self-regulatory behaviors in high-risk infants/toddlers, and improving overall EHS classroom quality. This study helps to fill the gap of research for promotion and prevention models with high-risk infants/toddlers, parents, and providers, as most research has been conducted on preschool and school-age students. The HI model needs more rigorous study, but provides hope for reducing disparities between impoverished children and their peers. This pilot study indicates the potential for success of the HI's promotion and prevention model, under "to-scale" expansions, at improving parent-infant interactions, reducing signs of atypical development in infants/toddlers, and improving the quality of EHS classrooms and teacher's caregiving practices. Given that there is limited research on the use of promotion and prevention models with high-risk parents and their infants/toddlers, further research is warranted. It would be crucial and beneficial to conduct a wider and more rigorous study using a group-randomized trial with a larger sample to further explore the benefits of promotion and prevention models, such as HI.

Author's Note

This research was supported in part with grants from the RK Mellon and Benedum Foundations of Pittsburgh. Correspondence concerning this article should be addressed to Tracy K. Larson, University of Pittsburgh, Pittsburgh, PA (tracy.larson@pitt.edu).

References

Bagnato, S. J., Neisworth, J. T., & Pretti-Frontczak, K. (2010). *Linking authentic assessment and early childhood interventions: Best measures for best practices (4th edition)*. Baltimore, MD: Paul Brookes Publishing Company.

Bagnato, S. J., Neisworth, J. T., Salvia, J., & Hunt, F. (1999). *Temperament and Atypical Behavior Scale (TABS); Early childhood indicators of developmental dysfunction: TABS assessment and intervention manual*. Baltimore, MD: Paul Brookes Publishing Company.

Bagnato, S. J., Neisworth, J. T., & Salvia, J. (1999). Normative detection of early regulatory disorders and autism: Confirmation of DC:0-3. *Infants and Young Children, 12*(2), 98-106.

Bagnato, S. J., Salaway, J., & Suen, H. K. (2009). *Pre-K counts in Pennsylvania for youngster's early school success: Authentic outcomes for an innovative prevention and promotion initiative.* Pittsburgh, PA: Early Childhood Partnerships; Children's Hospital of Pittsburgh of UPMC.

Bagnato, S. J., Seo, J. W., Salaway, J., & Kim, M. S. (2016). Field-validation of the COMET mentoring model to enhance the instructional practices of head start teachers. *Perspectives on Early Childhood Psychology and Education, 1*(1), 167-201.

Bagnato, S. J., Suen, H., Brantley, D., Smith-Jones, J., & Dettore, E. (2002). Child development impact of Pittsburgh's Early Childhood Initiative (ECI) in high-risk communities: First phase authentic evaluation research. *Early Childhood Research Quarterly, 17*(4), 559-580.

Biglan, A., Flay, B., Empty, D., & Sandler, I. (2012). The critical role of nurturing environments for promoting human wellbeing. *American Psychologist, 67*(4), 257-271.

Blair, C., & Raver, C. C. (2012). Child development in the context of adversity: Experiential canalization of brain and behavior. *American Psychologist, 67*(4), 309.

Centers for Disease Control (CDC). (2008). National survey of children with special health care needs 2005-2006.

Cook, T. D., & Campbell, D. T. (1979). *Quasi-experimentation: Design and analysis for field settings.* New York: Guilford Press, Inc.

Cook, G. A., & Roggman, L. A. (2009, January). PICCOLO (Parenting Interactions with Children: Checklist of Observations Linked to Outcomes) Technical Report. Logan, UT: Utah State University; Administration for Children, Youth, & Families, US Department of Health and Human Services, Washington, DC).

Crusto, C. A., Whitson, M. L., Feinn, R., Gargiulo, J., Holt, C., Paulicin, B., & Lowell, D. I. (2013). Evaluation of a mental health consultation intervention in preschool settings. *Best Practice in Mental Health, 9*(2), 1-21.

Felitti, V. J., Anda R. F., & Nordenberf, D. (1998). The relationship of adult status to childhood abuse and household dysfunction. *American Journal of Preventive Medicine, 14*, 245-258.

Fujiura, G. T., & Yamaki, K. (2005). Trends in the demography of childhood poverty and disability. *Exceptional Children, 66*(2), 187-199.

Gilliam, W. S., Maupin, A. N., & Reyes, C. R. (2016). Early childhood mental health consultation: Results of a statewide random-controlled evaluation. *Journal of the American Academy of Child & Adolescent Psychiatry, 55*(9), 754-761. doi:10.1016/j.jaac.2016.06.006.

Hemmeter, M. L. (2009). The Pyramid Infant Toddler Observation Scale (TPITOS). Retrieved from http://flfcic.fmhi.usf.edu/TACSEI/Evaluation/TPITOS.pdf. Center on the Social Emotional Foundations for Early Learning Technical Assistance Center on Social Emotional Interventions.

Hemmeter, M. L., Snyder, P., Fox, L., & Algina, J. (2016). Evaluating the implementation of the Pyramid Model for promoting social-emotional competence in early childhood classrooms. *Topics in Early Childhood Special Education, 17*, 1-14. doi:10.1177/0271121416653386.

Holub, C. K., Kershaw, T. S., Ethier, K. A., Lewis, J. B., Milan, S., & Ickovics, J. R. (2007). Prenatal and parenting stress on adolescent maternal adjustment: Identifying a high-risk subgroup. *Maternal & Child Health Journal, 11*(2), 153-159. doi:10.1007/s10995-006-0159-y

Lehman, C., Salaway, J., Bagnato, S.J., Grom, B., & Willard, B. (2010). Prevention as early intervention for young children at-risk: Recognition and response in early childhood. In Bray, M.A., & Kehle, T.J. (Eds.), *Oxford Handbook of School Psychology,* New York, NY.

Mayers, H. A., Hager-Budny, M., & Buckner, E. B. (2008). The chances for children teen parent–infant project: Results of a pilot intervention for teen mothers and their infants in inner city high schools. *Infant Mental Health Journal, 29*(4), 320-342. doi:10.1002/imhj.20182

McDonald, L., Conrad, T., Fairtlough, A., Fletcher, J., Green, L., Moore, L., & Lepps, B. (2009). An evaluation of a groupwork intervention for teen-age mothers and their families. *Child & Family Social Work, 14*(1), 45-57. doi:10.1111/j.1365-2206.2008.00580.x

Mollborn, S., Lawrence, E., James-Hawkins, L., & Fomby, P. (2014). How resource dynamics explain accumulating developmental and health disparities for teen parents' children. *Demography, 51*(4), 1199-1224. doi:10.1007/s13524-014-0301-1

National Center for Health Statistics. Healthy People 2010 Final Review. Hyattsville, MD. 2012

National Research Council and Institute of Medicine (2000) *From nerons to neighborhoods: The science of early childhood development.* Committee on Integrating the Science of Early Childhood Development. Jack P. Shonkoff and Deborah A. Phillips, (Eds.), Board on Children, Youth and Families, Commission on Behavioral and Social Sciences and Education. Washington, D.C.: National Academy Press.

Neisworth, J. T., Bagnato, S. J., & Hunt, F. (1999). *Temperament and Atypical Behavior Scale (TABS); Early childhood indicators of developmental dysfunction: TABS assessment and intervention manual.* Baltimore, MD: Paul Brookes Publishing Company.

Ocasio, K., Alst, D., Koivunen, J., Huang, C., & Allegra, C. (2015). Promoting preschool mental health: Results of a 3 year primary prevention strategy. *Journal of Child & Family Studies, 24*(6), 1800-1808. doi:10.1007/s10826-014-9983-7.

Ramey, C. T., & Ramey, S. L. (1998). Early intervention and early experience. *American Psychologist, 53*(2), 109.

Roggman, L. A., Cook, G. A., Innocenti, M. S., Jump, V. J. & Christiansen, K. (2013). *Parenting interactions with children: Checklist of observations linked to outcomes (PICCOLO) tool.* Baltimore, MD: Paul H. Brookes Publishing Co.

Shonkoff, J. P., & Garner, A. A. (2011). Toxic stress, brain development, and the early childhood foundations of lifelong health. *Pediatrics, 129*(1), 232-246.

Shonkoff., J. P., Richter, L., Vander Gaag, J., & Bhutta, Z. (2012) An integrated scientific framework for child survival and early childhood development. *Pediatrics, 129*(2). 345-358.

Smith, M., Gilmer, M., Salge, L., Dickerson, J., & Wilson, K. (2013). Who enrolls in teen parent education programs? An emphasis on personal and familial characteristics and services received. *Child & Adolescent Social Work Journal, 30*(1), 21-36. doi:10.1007/s10560-012-0276-y

Xue, Y., Boller K., Vogel C. A., Thomas, J., Caronongan, P., & Aikens, N. (2014). Early head start family and child experiences survey (Baby FACES) design options report (OPRE) report 2015-99. Washington, DC: Office of Planning, Research and Evaluation, Administration for Children and Families, U.S. Department of Health and Human Services.

Yoshikawa, H., Aber, J. L., & Beardslee, W. R. (2012). The effects of poverty on the mental, emotional, and behavioral health of children and youth: Implications for prevention. *American Psychologist, 67*(4), 272.

Supporting Increased Screening in the Pediatric Population

Laine Young-Walker, Melissa Stormont, Nathan Beucke, and Wendy Ell

Abstract

Early identification of developmental delays through developmental screening is critical for implementing early intervention. The American Academy of Pediatrics (AAP) recommends developmental screening across key areas (e.g., communication, gross motor, fine motor, social and emotional, and age-appropriate self-help) at 9, 18, and 24 or 30 months (Rice et al., 2014). In addition, children should be screened whenever a clinician's surveillance indicates risk. However, despite this recommendation, most pediatricians do not routinely screen their young patients. The goal of this study was to increase screening practices using a comprehensive evidence-based developmental screening tool among pediatricians in an academic based pediatric primary care clinic. Pediatricians included 42 resident physicians and 13 attending physicians (total n = 55) who were trained to screen children using the Ages and Stages Questionairre Third Edition (SQ-3) and Ages and Stages Questionairre - Social Emotional (ASQ-SE). Screenings were completed on all children ages 0-6 years in this pediatric practice at 9 month, 18 month, and 24 or 36 months well-child visits over a four year period of time. Over a four-year period, screenings by pediatricians in the participating county rose considerably from zero to 4256. Of these screenings, 4036 were ASQ screenings and 220 were ASQ-SE screenings. The pediatricians were provided with education and training on an evidence-based screening tool as well as strategies for addressing barriers to successfully implement the use of screening into their practice. One common barrier cited by pediatricians was a lack of direction for what to recommend when screening data indicate a need area. Therefore, this project also identified referral options.

Key Words: Developmental Screening, Pediatricians, Social-Emotional Screening, Ages and Stages Questionnaire (ASQ)

Developmental screening is critical for prevention and early intervention efforts. Approximately 15% to 18% of children in the United States have developmental or behavioral disabilities (Glascoe, 2000; Rice et al., 2014). Despite these prevalence statistics, childhood developmental and behavioral problems often go undetected and untreated; without the use of routine screening, up to 70% of children with needs are missed prior to their transition to kindergarten (Rice et al., 2014; Slomski, 2012). For certain groups, such as children born premature or from low socioeconomic status, early intervention has been shown to result in higher academic achievement (Mackrides & Ryherd, 2011). When properly applied, screening tests for developmental and behavioral problems in preschool children that are connected to early implementation of treatment can improve outcomes for children (Rice et al., 2014). Therefore, screening is supported by research as an essential practice to support young children at risk for various problematic outcomes.

The use of screening is also a recommended practice by national organizations that support best practices for young children. For example, in a 2006, revised 2010 policy statement, the American Association of Pediatrics (AAP) recommended that all children receive early identification services, including surveillance and screening, and if needed a developmental or diagnostic evaluation (Rice et al., 2014). The AAP recommends screening at 9, 18, and 24 or 30 months and the Center for Disease Control and Prevention (CDC) also emphasizes the importance of this area. "A current public health priority is to use early interventions to reduce, and ideally prevent, the occurrence and severity of long-term functional limitations" (Rice et al., 2014). In addition, children should be screened whenever a clinician's surveillance demonstrates risk. However, despite this recommendation, most pediatricians do not routinely screen their young patients (Council on Children With Disabilities [COCWD], 2006). This is concerning given research has documented that physicians have been shown to be poor at identifying children with developmental delays without the use of screening tools.

More recent evidence has documented that physicians are increasing the use of screening in their practice. For example, a study evaluating screening by pediatricians titled, "Trends in the Use of Standardized Tools for Developmental Screening in Early Childhood: 2002-2009," found the percentage of pediatricians using one or more screening tools more than doubled between 2002 and 2009 (from 23-47.7%) (Radecki, Sand-Loud, O'Connor, Sharp, & Olson, 2011). Despite this increase, more work to support efforts is clearly needed as approximately half of the pediatricians reported that they do not routinely use the recommended screening tools for patients younger than 36 months (Bethell, Reuland, Schor, Abrahms, & Halfon, 2011). To support increased use of screening practices, particularly for children under 3 years, more research on factors associated with use or barriers needs to be explored.

Some of the barriers to screening in pediatric practices include limited understanding of the importance of screening, time to complete the screening during office visits, lack of reimbursement for screening, and limited information on resources for referral of children with needs for support. Several of these barriers are overcome when pediatricians are aware of Child Find provisions and special Medicaid benefits for preventative health care for children enrolled in Medicaid. The Individuals with Disabilities Education Act (IDEA) mandates Child Find that requires schools to locate, identify, and evaluate all children with disabilities. Infants and toddlers with disabilities (birth to 2) receive early intervention services under IDEA Part C. Children and youth (ages 3-21 years) receive special education and related services under IDEA Part B (Wright & Wright, 2007). The Early and Periodic Screening, Diagnostic, and Treatment (EPSDT) benefit through Medicaid provides comprehensive and preventative health care services for children under age 21 who are enrolled in Medicaid. There is a federal law which requires that Medicaid cover a very comprehensive set of benefits and services for children. Despite Medicaid funding through EPSDT, many pediatricians are not aware that this service is reimbursable using the Current Procedural Terminology (CPT) billing code 96110 for developmental and behavioral screening.

In addition to these barriers, there are instances when screening does occur, but an evidence-based instrument is not utilized. Many pediatricians continue to rely on surveillance methods such as checklists and clinical observations that have poor sensitivity and can miss up to 45% of children with delays (Mackrides & Ryherd, 2011). There are evidence based screening tools that pediatricians can access and employ. The two most widely used evidence-based universal tools in primary care are the Ages & Stages Questionnaire - Third Edition (ASQ-3) and Parents Evaluation of Developmental Status (PEDS; Limbos & Joyce, 2011). The ASQ has a developmental screening (ASQ-3) and a social-emotional screening (ASQ-SE). The ASQ is a parent/caregiver completed screening tool with excellent psychometric properties including high test-retest (92% agreement) and interrater reliability (93% agreement), and item-scale internal consistency (Squires, Twambly, Bricker, & Potter, 2009). The ASQ also has strong concurrent validity and has been used successfully with a variety of populations (Dionne, McKinnon, Squires, & Clifford, 2014). It is critical that these tools are adopted by more individuals who are in a position to use them, including pediatricians. Further, it is also essential that there are more efforts made to increase pediatricians' use of evidence-based practices and address barriers, such as those in Table 1. It is also important to increase the coordination of links to resources based on community and state resources for children at risk according to screening data.

Summary and Purpose

Routine screening for developmental and social-emotional delays by pediatricians is critical for early identification, referrals, and early intervention. Providing a universal, evidence-based screening that can be used for all families is important in pediatric practices

Table 1:
Implementation Process in Clinical Setting

Aim: Practice will administer Ages and Stages Questionnaires at 9, 18, 24, and 30 month visits with an initial goal of 75% of well child checks and 90% of well child visits by 9 months post implementation

Determine work flow:
- Front office staff hands out forms to families
- Nursing collects form from family during rooming in process and attaches score sheet
- Physician scores before going into the room
- Physician discusses results with family
- Appropriate referrals made with documentation in the medical record

Required education for the clinic staff prior to implementation:
- Front office staff: Chart preparation of appropriate screening forms prior to patient arrival
- Nursing staff: Field questions from parents about items on the screening form
- Physicians: Scoring of the tool, using a referral algorithm and communicating results with families
- Billing and coding staff: Review of procedure codes for reimbursement

Development of a referral algorithm prior to implementation:
- Partner with local agencies providing early intervention services
- Determine capacity for services at local agencies

Chart review for process improvement:
- Evidence of completion rate
- Feedback to providers about appropriateness of referrals
- Ongoing support and education regarding the referral algorithm

for children under 6 years of age. Providing training, scoring, and interpretation of an evidence-based screening tool are factors, which will increase the likelihood of screening by pediatricians. This training will improve the knowledge of pediatricians, aid with implementation and interpretation, and remove a barrier, which limited screening. To this end, the purposes of this paper are first to describe how an interagency collaboration between pediatricians and an early child program supported increased screening practices with an evidence-based tool among pediatricians. A second purpose of this article is to discuss how barriers to screening were addressed, including adding a clear linkage between screening for risk and subsequent referral options.

Method

Participants

All 55 pediatricians who were invited to receive the training agreed to participate for an overall response rate of 100%. Pediatricians included 42 resident physicians and 13 attending physicians. All participating pediatricians received live in-person training to screen children using the ASQ-3 and ASQ-SE. These trainings occurred with residents during their required didactic schedule and attending physicians during their mandatory department meetings. After completion of trainings, screenings were completed on all children ages 0-6 years in the pediatric practice where these 55 pediatricians work at 9 month, 18 month, and 24 or 36 months well-child visits, which were documented over four year period of time.

Procedures and Intervention Implemented

Prior to initiation of the project, Institution Review Board approval was sought and the project found to be exempt. The county for the project is abbreviated to BC to blind the county. The BC Project LAUNCH (Linking Actions for Unmet Needs in

Children's Health) was funded by a five year grant (September 2010 to 2015) with a long term goal of fostering the healthy development and wellness of all young children in the target county from birth through age 8. One of the areas of focus for LAUNCH was to increase the use of developmental screenings in a range of child-serving settings. In 2011, the developers of the ASQ provided a train the trainer session, which includes extensive training of individuals to a level of proficiency with the assessment in order for these individuals to be able to train others. Subsequent to these sessions two pediatricians were able to deliver additional trainings on ASQ-3 and the ASQ-SE screenings to providers in the target county. ASQ kits were provided to those who were trained. The ASQ training also included training on how to link screening results to a local community referral matrix.

After completion of the initial training, two pediatricians completed multiple trainings of other pediatricians. Barriers to screening, which were identified by the pediatricians who would be delivering the screening, included: lack of knowledge and identification of an evidence based screening tool, the need for training in the ASQ-3 and ASQ-SE; the need for a process or strategy to embed screening into the clinical practice; the lack of knowledge of how to bill for screenings; and a lack of knowledge of referral sources for positive screens. These barriers were addressed in several ways. Discussion and education on the importance of an evidence-based screening tool occurred and buy-in to utilize the ASQ and ASQ-SE was obtained. Initially, the pediatricians were engaged in training to use the ASQ-3 and ASQ-SE. A strategy to embed screenings at 9 month, 18 month, and 24 or 36 months well-child visits was identified. The staff was trained on how to score and complete the summary page after screenings occurred. Office flow issues were problem solved for all of the participating pediatricians. In order to address these issues the LAUNCH team and the pediatricians discussed the challenges and determined that screenings would occur at well-child visits, following the AAP protocol (see Table 1). Education was provided to the pediatricians on billing Missouri Medicaid private insurances utilizing the EPSDT benefit. Also, connections were made with private insurers to determine how to bill for screenings that were completed. In order to address the barrier of lack of knowledge of referral sources a referral matrix was developed (see Table 2).

An academic-based pediatric primary care clinic was the largest pediatric population engaged in the intervention. A strong relationship between the LAUNCH team and the trained pediatricians within this department was built and a physician champion was identified to lead the efforts within the practice. This champion would deliver trainings and gather the support of other pediatricians to implement screening in their practice. This allowed the pediatricians to feel comfortable connecting with the team if any concerns arose. The training included suggestions on how to imbed the screening in their practice. The practice had to address readiness for change, which included addressing office flow and appropriate intervals to screen young children. After training, the lead pediatrician (champion) also reviewed screening results. If it was not clearly documented that they were using the referral tool, he would reach out to the individual provider.

Another important factor that had to be addressed was community resources for referrals. Identification of these resources was critical prior to the successful implementation of screening. In the absence of knowledge and easy access to referral resources, the pediatricians would likely have been frustrated when they identified children in need of services. A local referral matrix was created prior to any trainings occurring. The referral matrix was based on ASQ-3 and ASQ-SE results and helped guide decision-making and follow-up action. The matrix included a comprehensive community inventory of services and contact information to assist the provider (see Table 2).

Table 2:
Resources for Developmental & Social-Emotional Screening Referrals

ASQ-3 REFERRALS		ASQ-SE2 REFERRALS
HOME VISITING PROGRAMS	SPEECH	COUNSELING
Parents as teachers (0-5 yrs.): • Healthy families america •	Speech and hearing clinic • Women's and children's hospital • •	Behavioral health • Family counseling center • • Child psychology services •
DEVELOPMENTAL RESOURCES	VISION	
Title 1 preschool (3-5 yrs.): • • • First steps (0-3 yrs.) • • • Early childhood special education (3-5 yrs.) • • • • •	Free vision screenings for children • •	Child & adolescent clinic • Psychological services clinic •
	MOTOR SKILLS	
	Occupational therapy pediatric clinic • Free physical therapy clinic: •	
		PSYCHIATRY
		Child & adolescent clinic • Family counseling center • Behavioral health •
SOCIAL OPPORTUNITIES	HEARING	

• Local programs:
   •_____
   •_____
 • Play room & toy/resource check-out:
   •_____
	Audiology Clinic
	 •
	 Speech and hearing clinic
	 •
		ASSESSMENT

		• •
CASE MANAGEMENT & OTHER		

Results and Discussion

Barriers to Use of Screening

The initial training addressed: a) the lack of understanding of the importance of screening and, b) inadequate knowledge of a viable evidence-based screening tools. After training physicians on why and when to screen patients and the technical aspects of administering the screener (i.e., scoring and interpretation), the barriers to implementation in the office were addressed. Staff who would be utilized to complete screenings were identified and provided with education and training on the ASQ-3 and ASQ-SE. Potential disruptions to current patient flow were considered within the office with all 55 providers, the process for completion of screenings was identified, and costs/potential reimbursement was solved. Utilizing AAP guidelines, it was determined that completion of screenings would occur at 9 month, 18 month, and 24 or 36 months well-child visits.

Impact: Screening

Prior to the intervention no pediatricians in the BC academic based pediatric primary care clinic were using any comprehensive evidence-based developmental screening tool. After the 55 pediatricians were trained, screenings were performed at all well-child visits - 9 month, 18 month, and 24 or 36 month. Screenings completed from 2011 to 2015 were tracked. During the four-year period, the use of screening by pediatricians in the participating county rose considerably from zero to a total of 4256 over a period of 4 years. Regarding the screening tools used, for the vast majority, 4036 were the ASQ; only 220 children were screened using the ASQ-SE.

Linkages Based on Results

After screening occurred, there was a clear need for increased efforts to provide guidance for referrals. At least 75% of the pediatricians in the practice stated to the third author that historically they did not complete screening due to a lack of information regarding referral resources once screening indicated a problem in a mental health area. Through working with pediatricians, the third author brought these concerns to the grant team working to support increased screening in the area. The team created a referral matrix for the pediatricians to utilize in referring these young children to local resources. There were discussions and decisions made as to who would make referrals and a strategy to monitor them was created. Referrals based on screening results were made for 318 of the ASQ screens and 41 of the ASQ-SEs. Often in the medical field, change in recommended practices is not implemented with careful consideration of logistical considerations, which can quickly undermine the use of new practices. In Table 1 we articulate the way in which the third author provided support for his clinical practice and other attendings on practical implications. There are several needs to support effective implementation of new practices. It is also imperative to secure one person to help lead and coach others by providing feedback on screening implementation and problem solving through barriers.

Conclusion

Developmental, behavioral, and emotional problems are quite common in childhood. Often these problems and delays go undetected. In this article an example was provided of how one county partnered with a local university department to support screening of children during critical early development. This federally funded partnership provided education and training on an evidence-based screening tool (ASQ-3 and ASQ-SE) and a strategy for addressing barriers to implementation, which was associated with increased screenings in the pediatric population. Overall, the routine use of screening with the ASQ was adopted successfully within the practice. Historically, this academic-based pediatric primary care clinic functioned independently.

After the LAUNCH grant was implemented they joined in a partnership with the pediatric primary care clinic. As a result of this partnership, the number of comprehensive evidence-based developmental screenings increased from zero to over 4,000 in 4 years. Developmental and social–emotional screenings were completed using the ASQ and ASQ-SE. There was a significantly lower percentage of children screened using the ASQ-SE. Although screening for social-emotional development using the ASQ-SE was slower to implement, the practice is now implementing universal ASQ-SE screening at the 12-month and 3 year well-child checks. Future needs for pediatric screening include determining barriers related to screening for social-emotional development and workforce development in early childhood. One of the potential barriers could be the lack of mental health providers with expertise in working with young children to explain differences between normal development and concerns. Furthermore, more awareness is needed among professionals who screen young children to reduce stigma around mental health.

Author's Note:

Correspondence regarding this article may be sent to Laine Young-Walker, MD, Department of Psychiatry, MA 204 Medical Sciences Building, Columbia MO 65212, (573) 882-2923, YoungWalkerL@health.missouri.edu. This work was supported by the Substance Abuse and Mental Health Services Administration (SAMHSA) grant number: 5H79SM060226-03

References

Bethell, C., Reuland, C., Schor, E., Abrahms, M., & Halfon, F. (2011). Rates of parent-centered developmental screening: Disparities and links to services access. *Pediatrics, 128*, 146-155.

Council on Children with Disabilities (2006). Identifying infants and young children with developmental disorders in the medical home: An algorithm for developmental surveillance and screening. *Pediatrics, 118*, 405-420.

Dionne, C., McKinnon, S., Squires, J., & Clifford J. (2014). Developmental screening in a Canadian First Nation (Mohawk): Psychometric properties and adaptations of ages & stages questionnaires (2nd edition). *BMC Pediatrics, 14*, 14-23.

Glascoe, F. P. (2000). Early detection of developmental and behavioral problems. *Pediatrics in Review. 21*, 272-280.

Limbos, M. M., & Joyce, D. P. (2011). Comparison of the ASQ and PEDS in screening for developmental delay in children presenting for primary care. *Journal of Developmental and Behavioral Pediatrics, 32*, 499-511.

Mackrides, P. S., & Ryherd, S. J. (2011). Screening for developmental delay. *American Family Physician, 84*, 544-549.

Radecki, L., Sand-Loud N., O'Connor, K. G., Sharp, S., & Olson, L. M. (2011). Trends in the use of standardized tools for developmental screening in early childhood: 2002-2009. *Pediatrics, 128*(1), 14-19.

Rice, C. E., Braun, K.V., Kogan, M.D., Smith, C., Kavanagh, Strickland, B., & Blumberg, S. J. (2014, September). Screening for developmental delays among young children-National survey of children's health, United States, 2007. *Morbidity and Mortality Weekly Report, 63*(2), 27-35. Retrieved from https://www.cdc.gov/mmwr/preview/mmwrhtml/su6302a5.htm

Slomski, A. (2012). Chronic mental health issues in children now loom larger than physical problems. *Journal of the American Medical Association, 308*, 223-225.

Squires, J., Twambly, E., Bricker, D., & Potter, L. (2009). *ASQ-3 user's guide.* Baltimore, MD: Paul H. Brookes Publishing Co, Inc.

Wright, P. W. D., & Wright, P. D. (2007). *Wrightslaw: Special education law* (2nd ed). Hartfield, VA: Habor House Law Press.

Equity-Based Practices in Early Childhood: The Role of the School Psychologist

Brandy L. Clarke, Kristin M. Rispoli, Nicholas W. Gelbar, Evelyn Bilias-Lolis, and Melissa A. Bray

Abstract

The early childhood developmental period has gained significant emphasis in research and practice as an important period for educational programming and policy. Research outcomes continue to demonstrate a host of long-term academic, social-emotional, and health benefits for students who participate in high quality early learning programs. Such programs, however, are not universally accessible thereby excluding a critical mass of students due to financial disadvantage. This manuscript explored the current landscape of early childhood education and care within the context of raising awareness for equity-based practices and equal access for all students. The school psychologist is an educational professional who assumes a critical role in this process.

Key Words: early childhood, poverty, equity, school psychology, high-quality early education

There is consensus in the field of early childhood that the early years of a child's life have a critical impact on his/her developmental trajectory across all domains. Specifically, research on early brain development has revealed that infants develop nearly 700 new neural connections per second in their first few years of life (Shonkoff, Boyce, & McEwen, 2009). These connections are highly influenced by environmental stimulation and relationships formed with early caregivers. Children who are nurtured in stimulating environments surrounded by responsive caregivers are more likely to develop the cognitive, social-emotional, and behavioral skills needed for optimal outcomes, including academic achievement and social-emotional well-being (Landry, Smith, & Swank, 2006; Treyvaud et al., 2009). On the other hand, young children who experience biological insults or malformations, environmental deprivation, and/or disengaged attachments with caregivers are likely to experience delays or disabilities. These delays negatively impact their developmental progression and, without intervention, will likely persist into adulthood (Shonkoff & Marshall, 2000).

The period of early childhood is often conceptualized as ranging from birth to age 8 years (National Association for the Education of Young Children [NAEYC], 1997). During this period, children experience bouts of rapid growth and development across all domains – physical, cognitive, social-emotional, and behavioral. Delays or disabilities in any one area can have compounding effects across all others. For example, an infant who experiences delays in language development may also experience cognitive delays (e.g., decreased vocabulary and concept formation), as well as social delays due to an inability to communicate with peers and adults (Hart & Risley, 1995). Although slower rates of language acquisition may appear to represent a small difference between children, if left unaddressed, these gaps may continue to increase over time and become more difficult to correct (Dale, Price, Bishop, & Plomin, 2003; Hoff, 2013). In other words, even though children with early delays may continue to improve in their skill development, without early intervention to boost skill attainment, the gap between them and their peers will become larger over time and they may always remain behind (Entwisle, 1995). Thus, there is a critical need to support the early learning experiences and development of young children to provide a foundation for optimal, enduring outcomes. This is especially so for young children from impoverished backgrounds who often need extra support to access quality educational services.

Support for Early Education and Intervention Programs

High quality early education and intervention programs designed to identify children at-risk for deleterious outcomes and ameliorate these negative conditions have had profound positive and long-lasting effects, not only for the young children, but also for society at large (Anderson et al., 2003; Barnett, 2000; Ramey & Ramey, 2004). Longitudinal studies revealed that high quality programs have positive short-term effects on children's pre-academic skills, social-emotional and behavioral functioning, and relational attachments (Heckman, Moon, Pinto, Savelyev, & Yavitz, 2010; Karoly, Kilburn, & Cannon, 2005; Masse & Barnett, 2002). Furthermore, these programs positively influence long-term outcomes, such as completing high school, increased rates of employment influencing community tax bases, and overall physical and mental health (Heckman et al., 2010). For example, a review of the collective randomized clinical trials of the ABC/Abecedarian Project have consistently revealed positive outcomes for young children enrolled in the early learning program compared to children who were not enrolled, including higher IQ and achievement scores, greater social competencies, higher levels of academic achievement over time, and greater adult employment (Ramey & Ramey, 2004). Not only do these research findings reveal strong effects of early education and intervention on important child outcomes, but also significant economic benefits as well. Estimated returns on investments in high quality early childhood programming are as high as $9 returned for every $1 invested (Heckman et al., 2010.). These investments also yield decreases in special education, custodial care, and incarceration costs producing impressive investments for the public (Heckman et al., 2010).

Despite these positive findings, some programs have been less successful or have not been able to produce conclusive evidence of their effects for addressing achievement gaps for children at-risk for school failure (Ramey & Ramey, 1998, 2004). Historically, early research into Head Start programming produced inconsistent findings to support its national benefit (U.S. General Accounting Office, 1997). Recently, a randomized control trial of Head Start was conducted through the Head Start Impact Study wherein data from 5,000 newly entering 3- and 4-year-old children were gathered from fall of 2002 through 2006 (U.S. Department of Health and

Human Services Administration for Children and Families, 2010). Comparisons were made of children participating in Head Start versus a control group participating in other early childhood programs to determine the impacts of Head Start on children's school readiness and parental practices supporting optimal child development. The study also sought to determine under which circumstances and for which children Head Start had the greatest impact. Overall, the study revealed that across nearly every measure, the Head Start group experienced more positive results than the control group; however, few of those benefits were maintained through the end of first grade. Additionally, subgroup findings indicated that there were inconsistent effects, some of which were negative, where children of parents with moderate symptoms of depression experienced negative impacts of Head Start across cognitive, social-emotional, and health domains, and mixed results on parenting practices through first grade. Additionally, white children in the 4-year-old cohort showed negative impacts on teacher ratings of social-emotional measures in first grade and a negative impact on parenting behaviors in kindergarten. By way of example, this study further illustrates the need for continued research in the area of early childhood programming to elucidate those aspects of high quality programs that lead to optimal outcomes.

It has been hypothesized that those early childhood programs that were found to be ineffective at producing positive gains may have lacked the necessary preservice/inservice teacher training to promote high quality education or that there may be inadequate intensity of services to meet students' needs. Additionally, they may have employed a remedial rather than preventive focus or provided more family support than direct teaching to the child (Ramey & Ramey, 2004). Further research is needed to determine what factors produce positive benefits and for whom.

Defining High Quality

Concerted efforts to define and design standards for developing the physical, cognitive, emotional, and social competencies of preschool children are visible both locally in the United States and internationally. In the United States, in order to determine what constitutes "high quality" programming, committees of expert researchers and practitioners conducted a review of the current literature on evidence-based strategies and best recommendations in the field resulting in standards of practice. The National Association for the Education of Young Children (NAEYC) has established ten standards of high-quality early childhood education that serve as their accreditation criteria for high-quality programs (NAEYC, 2006). These criteria include: a) promoting positive relationships for all children and adults, b) implementing a curriculum focused on all domains of child development, c) using developmentally, culturally, and linguistically appropriate and effective teaching practices, d) utilizing ongoing assessments of children's progress, e) fostering the health and nutrition of children and staff, f) employing and supporting qualified personnel, g) establishing and maintaining collaborative relationships with families, h) establishing and maintaining relationships and utilizing resources in the community, i) providing a safe and healthy physical environment, and j) implementing effective program management that results in high-quality service. The rigorous NAEYC accreditation system has established a method for defining and evaluating high-quality early childhood programs; however, at this time the program is voluntary.

The Division for Early Childhood (DEC) of the Council for Exceptional Children (CEC) has also developed a list of recommended practices to provide guidance to practitioners and families regarding the most effective ways to support young children, birth through age five years, who have or are at-risk for developmental delays or disabilities, especially those from disadvantaged environments (Division for Early Childhood, 2014). These recommendations are designed to bridge the gap between research in evidence-based interventions and their translation into practice. They are also drawn from the best wisdom and experience available in the field. The topical areas addressed in the recommendations include a) leadership, b) assessment, c) environment, d) family, e) instruction, f) interaction, g) teaming and collaboration, and h) transition. Within each topical area, the division has established a list of recommended practices specified for practitioners in the field serving young children with special needs. Collectively, the NAEYC accreditation standards and the DEC recommended practices form a foundation upon which to define and identify high quality early education and intervention services that may promote optimal learning outcomes for all young children.

Likewise, at the more global level, early childhood education and care (ECEC) has become a policy priority in many countries across the world with a number of countries devising standards and monitoring systems to ensure accountability in ECEC (oecd. org). Several international agencies such as the Organization for Economic Co-Operation and Development (OECD), United Nations Educational Scientific and Cultural Organization (UNESCO), UNICEF, and the European Union have developed guidelines on high quality programming based on comparisons and/or ratings between and amongst countries. The literature in this area suggests that quality is the most important variable contributing to the degree and impact of ECEC; although there remain varying perspectives on what constitutes quality (Wall, Litjens, & Taguma, 2015). Common to most perspectives is the notion that quality has structural and process components. Structural quality involves factors that relate to the structure of the classroom, student-teacher ratios, faculty qualifications, etc.; while process refers to the contextual variables such as the interactions the young child experiences with his/her direct environment, as well as good pedagogy (Wall et al., 2015).

Contributions to Inequity in the Field

Despite the success and overwhelming evidence supporting high quality early education and intervention programs, widespread implementation of high quality programming has not been achieved for all children. Funding for programs varies widely from state to state and district to district. Providing consistent educational and intervention programs requires a collaborative effort of federal, state, and private dollars. With varied funding sources, expectations and regulations for how such dollars can be spent, and the availability of funds is inconsistent. Given the limited funding, programs have to make sacrifices in the quality of programming provided, staff hired, and expand eligibility criteria for enrollments outside of program expertise. Thus, variability in funding can create potential disparities in the availability of high quality programming from community to community, state to state, and, sadly, from child to child.

Another factor likely underlying inequality in early childhood education is differential program impact. Program evaluation research is sorely needed to determine which programs are most effective at producing favorable outcomes and for whom; however, implications and generalizations from such work are difficult to ascertain due to the irregularity in the implementation of standard practices (Meisels & Shonkoff, 2000). In other words, it is difficult to determine the efficacy of early childhood programs and interventions if they are not implemented or received as intended. An additional challenge in program evaluation research is the disparity in the length and intensity of services, such as delivery of full-day or part-day programming, and the number of days programs operate (year-round versus academic year, 5 days a week versus 3-4 days a week).

Early Childhood Education and Poverty: A Twofold Gap

The effects of poverty on early learning can manifest in a twofold way: 1) effects on access to preschool and subsequent opportunities to learn, and 2) effects on specific cognitive, academic, socioemotional, and physical developmental domains despite access to preschool programming.

Issues of Access and Equity

Shifts in early childhood practices have been and continue to be heavily influenced by public policies. Funds were initially distributed to initialize early childhood special education and teacher-training programs under Public Law 90-538 and Project Head Start in the late 1960s. In the 1990s, the passing of Public Law 99-457 and Part B of the Individuals with Disabilities Education Act (IDEA), afforded children aged 3 to 5 years similar rights to free and appropriate public education and special education services. They also provided incentives to states to offer services for infants and toddlers identified with disabilities and their families. Updates in IDEA 2004 have maintained the focus on serving young children with special needs and their families in special education regulations. However, many still believe that young children from impoverished families are not being adequately and equitably served under the law.

Nonetheless, the importance of high quality early education for *all* children is now increasingly recognized and is influencing policies developed at the local, state, national, and international arenas. For example, the Obama administration's Preschool for All initiative was an attempt to curb "opportunity gaps" through universal preschools. Collaborations among the U.S. Department of Health and Human Services (HHS) and the U.S. Department of Education were focused on significantly expanding and improving early education services for all children and families. Included in the proposed plans were expansions in a) high-quality infant and toddler care through Early Head Start-child care partnerships, b) voluntary evidence-based home visitation to vulnerable families, and c) voluntary, high-quality, full-day preschool for 4-year-olds living at or below 200% of the federal poverty line. These expansions increased the pool of federal funding and created a more competitive market for early childhood programs.

To date, however, the option of universal, high quality public preschool is not uniformly available in the United States (Wright, 2011). Although recent legislative efforts are underway to create a more equitable process, children entering kindergarten today can range from those who attended formal programming opportunities starting as early as age 2 years on one extreme to those who did not attend preschool at all. Children residing in poverty are the most negatively impacted in states where universal programming and subsidized care through Head Start or other social welfare programs are not available, requiring parents to finance the tuition for private preschool programs (Wright, 2011) or to forgo them altogether. Likewise, prekindergarten enrollment disparities exist between varying Socio-Economic Stress (SES) levels as well as geographic region. Barnett and Yarosz (2007) found that 55% of children living in homes with a family income ranging between $20,000-30,000 U.S. dollars were enrolled in formal preschool programs as opposed to 84% of their peers from homes with incomes ranging from $75,000-100,000. Enrollment trends between urban and rural geographic regions have indicated that children growing up in rural areas are less likely to attend preschool when compared to children in urban areas (Wright, 2011) and that 52% of children raised in the West were likely to be enrolled in prekindergarten as opposed to 37% of children in the Northeast (Child Trends, 2010).

Effects of Poverty on Preschoolers' Cognitive, Emotional, and Socio-Behavioral Development

Poverty directly impacts child development. Preschoolers from families of low income often enter school behind their peers in all areas of academics and exhibit greater rates of behavioral concerns (Allhusen, Belsky, & Booth-La-Force, 2005). Fortunately, intervention programs have shown promise in helping disadvantaged preschoolers catch up to their peers academically and lower their risk of long-term deleterious outcomes (Herman-Smith, 2013). Programs such as the HighScope Perry Preschool Project, Chicago Child-Parent Centers, and Carolina Abecedarian Project were very successful in increasing academic achievement scores on standardized testing, decreasing school dropout rates, decreasing criminal acts, and improving student behavior in schools and within the community (Herman-Smith, 2013) as demonstrated via longitudinal data collected on participants through young adulthood..

Opportunities for School Psychologists in Increasing Access and Equity for Young Children in Poverty

Understanding the current landscape and the issues facing the field of early childhood is important to school psychologists who seek to increase access and equity in the provision of early learning and intervention services for children living in poverty. School psychologists possess breadth and depth in knowledge relevant to supporting the diverse needs of young learners including assessment techniques across academic, social-emotional, and behavioral domains, evidence-based intervention strategies to support child functioning across home and school settings, and consultation techniques for supporting individual and systems-level change. The primary service modalities by which school psychologists practice (i.e., assessment, treatment, and consultation) offer numerous opportunities for increasing the availability of specialized educational and mental health supports and promoting broad changes that serve to advocate for the needs of young children whose families may otherwise face substantial barriers to obtaining such services outside of the school system.

Studies highlighting the importance of high quality education in promoting school readiness for children from low-SES environments point to the need for communication between early educators and elementary schools, such that knowledge of expectations and sharing of information can occur across both settings to promote readiness for children at risk of early school failure (Fantuzzo et al., 2005). Given the broad training in assessment, treatment and consultation, school psychologists are ideally positioned to foster such communication to ensure that the transition across programming promotes success for children in poverty.

Assessment

It is essential that assessment practices in early childhood make use of developmentally-appropriate, sensitive measures that account for the unique contributions of children's environments and background characteristics. School psychologists are specially trained in understanding the role that variations in development and environment may play when conducting assessment and interpreting results (Bagnato, 2006; National Association of School Psychologists, 2009). School psychologists may train early childhood staff on the use of psychometrically sound measures, oversee the interpretation of results (including to what degree culture and family background may have contributed to results), and collaborate on subsequent educational decision making to determine whether vulnerable students are demonstrating adequate progress toward kindergarten readiness and/or receiving appropriate supports for their mental health and behavioral needs.

The determination of readiness for kindergarten entry, a primary focus of early childhood assessment, is complicated by the lack of consensus regarding the skills that constitute readiness (Wakabayashi & Beal, 2015). Practices to assess for these skills subsequently vary between states and within communities (Wakabayashi & Beal, 2015). Assessment protocols may fail to account for discrepancies between the availability of and exposure to high-quality early education programs across both states and communities with differential access to economic resources and support for such programming. To combat this trend, school psychologists should serve as leaders in the implementation of comprehensive assessment systems that align with the recommendations of the Early Childhood Education

State Assessment Collaborative, including the use of culturally sensitive, multi-domain, multi-method assessment that incorporates input from several sources (Howard, 2011). Similar to standards for a comprehensive assessment, school psychologists should ensure parent and teacher opinion/observation, medical history, and school performance (Gredler, 2000) are included when working with at-risk families (Reynolds & Kamphaus, 2003).

Identification

School psychologists evaluating individual students should ensure children from low SES backgrounds are included in the standardized assessment measures used for decision-making. In this role, the school psychologist should assist the team in determining to what degree the child's unique risk factors and life circumstances (e.g., degree of exposure to a rich and stimulating home environment) may affect the interpretation of findings. For example, outcomes resulting from constricted exposure and limited opportunities to learn should be qualified as such in assessment reports and in intervention planning efforts.

Intervention/Consultation

An estimated 20% of children living in poverty are reported to exhibit behavioral issues in the preschool years (Holtz, Fox, & Meurer, 2015). Consultation services aimed at improving parenting practices and teacher behavior management buffer the effects of problematic behavior among young children by increasing the parents' and educators' ability to use preventive and intervention strategies in an effective manner (Alkon, Ramler, & MacLennan, 2003; Amini-Virmani et al., 2013). Regular provision of Early Childhood Mental Health Consultation (ECMHC) is associated with reduced expulsion of young children enrolled in prekindergarten centers (Gilliam, 2005) and can ensure access to behavioral health services for children living in poverty, who may otherwise lack connections to these resources outside of the school setting.

School psychologists can serve as leaders in the implementation of ECMHC, providing coordination of hiring, training, and ongoing supervision of consultants working in early childhood settings. Consultation delivered by school employees provides the opportunity for frequent, ongoing meetings between teachers and consultants, two characteristics that predict ECMHC success (Amini-Virmani et al., 2013; Carlson, et al., 2012). School psychologists are also well-prepared to oversee other aspects of high-quality ECMHC such as clarifying the consultation model based on child needs, maintaining ongoing data collection with psychometrically sound instruments, establishing relationships with collaborating agencies and encouraging ongoing communication, and providing assistance to program sites (Carlson et al., 2012).

Children of low-income families require close collaborative engagements with school-based practitioners that understand their children within the context of their environment and persist in their efforts to innovatively push through barriers in order to create access. Consultation can involve coordination of collaboration, communication, outreach, and advocacy in order to raise social and legislative consciousness around matters unique to the population. Equity-based practices for ECEC involves consultative expertise that permeates the educational system and with this, the larger community. School psychologists must work sensitively to understand, advocate for, and meet the needs of such learners in order to empower families, educators, and communities to do the same.

School psychologists also serve as an integral member of the early childhood team by evaluating the usefulness of interventions and determining what resources might provide the most appropriate supports for children living in poverty. Equity-based practices require an ability to identify practices that have a sufficient evidence base to support their use with children from low-SES environments, and engaging in effective evaluation practices to determine their effectiveness for the individual child.

Family Engagement

School psychologists may play a direct role in facilitating relationships between parents and teachers through the implementation of family-focused practices (e.g., Sheridan, Clarke, Knoche, & Pope-Edwards, 2006). These efforts are of considerable importance given research highlighting the role of positive parent-teacher relationships in promoting parent involvement in early education for families living in poverty (Mendez, 2010). Family engagement is paramount to the school success of children born into poverty (Cooper & Crosnoe, 2007; Kingston, Huang, Calzada, Dawson-McClure, & Brotman, 2013), yet families living in poverty often report lower levels of involvement compared to their higher income counterparts (Cooper & Crosnoe, 2007; Waanders, Mendez, & Downer, 2007). Family-centered interventions focus not only on what services are provided to the family and the child, but the manner in which families are engaged to support parents in acquiring the competence and confidence to foster their own child's development (Dunst & Trivette, 2009). Thus, services are designed and implemented in a fashion that not only meet the needs of the individual child, but also meet the needs and situation of the family. Using these recommended practices, interventions are based on the strengths and assets of the child and family to support their parental autonomy and capabilities, as well as family culture, preferences, and values.

Several logistical barriers need to be considered when working to engage familiar of low income. Parents with low-income often work more than one job in order to provide for their families and full-time work is associated with lower levels of parental involvement in education among families living below the poverty line (Castro, Bryant, Peisner-Feinberg & Skinner, 2004).Limitations such as transportation difficulties, competing commitments, and/or a lack of alternative childcare options can impede family engagement efforts (Mendez, 2010). School psychologists thus have a responsibility to raise awareness around these practical considerations when planning for instruction and intervention opportunities that involve parental input and support. Examples of culturally sensitive planning strategies can include the provision of public transportation tokens to meet appointments, accommodations for babysitting/childcare, as well as home visits that maximize engagement and school-home collaboration efforts.

Conclusion

High quality early learning experiences for vulnerable young children are critical to supporting their optimal growth, development, and success. More research is needed to understand what factors constitute "high quality" programming and for whom such programming is most effective. Despite the need for further research, school psychologists can still play a role in helping to promote equitable access to early learning opportunities for young children living in poverty.

While calls for increased involvement of school psychologists in early childhood have primarily been communicated through the research literature, it is believed that these aspirations will soon be realized given increased attention across the nation to early childhood education and care (McIntyre, Eckert, Arbolino, Reed, & Fiese, 2014). Several opportunities exist for school psychologists to lend their expertise in the early childhood arena. In particular, school psychologists can serve as leaders, collaborators, and direct agents in implementing assessment, intervention, and consultation to enhance the educational experience of young, vulnerable children.

Though the research reviewed above highlights several ways in which school psychologists may serve early childhood settings, more research is needed to examine the specific ways in which school psychological services can maximize young children's personal and academic growth from age through 8 years of age, particularly for children living in poverty. Globally, investigations are needed to methodically examine the ability of school psychologists to obtain and transfer this knowledge across countries and continents in a socially just and equitable way. Certainly, there is enough traction, momentum, and interest in research, training, and practice to commit to such a cause.

References

Alkon, A., Ramler, M., & MacLennan, K. (2003). Evaluation of mental health consultation in child care centers. *Early Childhood Education Journal, 31,* 91-99.

Allhusen, V., Belsky, J., & Booth-La-Force, C. (2005). Duration and developmental timing of poverty and children's cognitive and social development from birth through third grade. *Child Development, 76,* 795-810. doi:10.1111/j.1467-8624.2005.00878.x

Amini-Virmani, E. Amini, Masyn, K. E., Thompson, R. A., Conners-Burrow, N. A., & Whiteside-Mansell, L. (2013). Early childhood mental health consultation: Promoting change in the quality of teacher–child interactions. *Infant Mental Health Journal, 34*(2), 156–172. doi:10.1002/imhj.21358

Anderson, L. M., Shinn, C., Fullilove, M. T., Scrimshaw, S. C., Fielding, J. E., Normand, J., & Carande-Kulis, V. G. (2003). The effectiveness of early childhood development programs: A systematic review. *American Journal of Preventive Medicine, 24,* 32-46. Retrieved from http://dx.doi.org/10.1016/S0749-3797(02)00655-4

Bagnato, S. J. (2006). Of helping and measuring for early childhood intervention: Reflections on issues and school psychology's role. *School Psychology Review, 35*(4), 615–620.

Barnett, W. S. (2000). Economics of early childhood intervention. In J. P. Shonkoff & S. J. Meisels (Eds.), *Handbook of early childhood intervention-Second edition* (pp. 589-610). New York, NY: Cambridge University Press.

Barnett, W.S., & Yarosz, D.J. (2007). *Who goes to preschool and why does it matter? (NIEER Policy Brief, 15).* Rutgers, NJ: National Institute for Early Education Research.

Carlson, J. S., Mackrain, M. A., van Egeren, L. A., Brophy-Herb, H., Kirk, R. H., Marciniak, D., & Tableman, B. (2012). Implementing a statewide early childhood mental health consultation approach to preventing childcare expulsion. *Infant Mental Health Journal, 33*(3), 265–273. Retrieved from http://dx.doi.org.proxy2.cl.msu.edu/10.1002/imhj.21336

Castro, D. C., Bryant, D. M., Peisner-Feinberg, E. S., & Skinner, M. L. (2004). Parent involvement in Head Start programs: The role of parent, teacher and classroom characteristics. *Early Childhood Research Quarterly, 19,* 413-430. doi:10.1016/j.ecresq.2004.07.005

Child Trends. (2010). *Early childhood program enrollment.* Retrieved from http://www.childtrends.org/indicators/early-childhood-program-enrollment/

Cooper, C. E., & Crosnoe, R. (2007). The engagement in schooling of economically disadvantaged parents and children. *Youth & Society, 38,* 372-391. doi: 10.1177/0044118X06289999

Dale, P. S., Price, T. S., Bishop, D. V. M., & Plomin, R. (2003). Outcomes of early language delay: Predicting persistent and transient language difficulties at 3 and 4 years. *Journal of Speech, Language, and Hearing Research, 46,* 544-560. doi:10.1044/1092-4388(2003/044)

Division for early childhood. (2014). *DEC recommended practices in early intervention/early childhood special education 2014.* Retrieved from http://www.dec-sped.org/recommendedpractices.

Dunst, C. J., & Trivette, C. M. (2009). Capacity-building family-systems intervention practices. *Journal of Family Social Work, 12*(2), 119-143.

Entwisle, D. R. (1995). The role of schools in sustaining benefits of early childhood programs. *The Future of Children, 5,* 133-144.

Fantuzzo, J. W., Rouse, H. L., McDermott, P. A., Sekino, Y., Childs, S., & Weiss, A. (2005). Early childhood experiences and kindergarten success: A population-based study of a large urban setting. *School Psychology Review, 34,* 571-588.

Gilliam, W. S. (2005). *Prekindergarteners left behind: Expulsion rates in state prekindergarten systems.* New York, NY: Foundation for Child Development.

Gredler, G. R. (2000). Early childhood education—assessment and intervention: What the future holds. *Psychology in the Schools, 37*(1), 73-79.

Hart, B., & Risley, T. R. (1995). *Meaningful differences in the everyday experience of young American children.* Baltimore, MD: Paul H Brookes Publishing.

Heckman, J. J., Moon, S. H., Pinto, R., Savelyev, P. A., & Yavitz, A. (2010). The rate of return to the High/Scope Perry Preschool Program. *Journal of Public Economics, 94*(1-2), 114–128.

Herman-Smith, R. (2013). Do preschool programs affect social disadvantage? What social workers should know. *Social Work, 58*(1), 65-73.

Hoff, E. (2013). Interpreting the early language trajectories of children from low-SES and language minority homes: Implications for closing achievement gaps. *Developmental Psychology, 49*(1), 4.

Holtz, C. A., Fox, R. A., & Meurer, J. R. (2015). Incidence of behavior problems in toddlers and preschool children from families living in poverty. *The Journal of Psychology, 149,* 161-174. doi:10.1080/00223980.2013.853020

Howard, E. C. (2011). *Moving forward with kindergarten readiness assessment efforts: A position paper of the Early Childhood Education State Collaborative on assessment and student standards.* Council of Chief State School Officers. Retrieved from http://eric.ed.gov.proxy1.cl.msu.edu/?id=ED543310

Karoly, L. A., Kilburn, R.M., & Cannon, J. (2005). *Early childhood interventions: Proven results, future promise.* RAND Corporation.

Kingston, S., Huang, K. Y., Calzada, E., Dawson-McClure, S., & Brotman, L. (2013). Parent involvement in education as a moderator of family and neighborhood socioeconomic context on school readiness among young children. *Journal of Community Psychology, 41,* 265–276. doi:10.1002/jcop.21528

Landry, S. H., Smith, K. E., & Swank, P. R. (2006). Responsive parenting: establishing early foundations for social, communication, and independent problem-solving skills. *Developmental Psychology, 42*(4), 627.

Masse, L. N., & Barnett, W. S. (2002). A benefit-cost analysis of the Abecedarian early childhood intervention. In H.M. Lewin & P.J. McEcwan (Eds.), *Cost-Effectiveness and Educational Policy,* (pp. 152-173)Larchmont, *NY: Eye on Education, Inc.*

McIntyre, L. L., Eckert, T. L., Arbolino, L. A., Reed, F. D. D., & Fiese, B. H. (2014). The transition to kindergarten for typically developing children: A survey of school psychologists' involvement. *Early Childhood Education Journal, 42*(3), 203–210. doi:10.1007/s10643-013-0593-6

Meisels, S. J., & Shonkoff, J. P. (2000). Early childhood intervention: A continuing evolution. In J. P. Shonkoff & S. J. Meisels (Eds.), *Handbook of early childhood intervention-second edition* (pp. 3-31). New York, NY: Cambridge University Press.

Mendez, J. L. (2010). How can parents get involved in preschool? Barriers and engagement in education by ethnic minority parents of children attending Head Start. *Cultural Diversity and Ethnic Minority Psychology, 16,* 26-36. doi:10.1037/a0016258

NAEYC. (2006). *Introduction to the NAEYC accreditation standards and criteria.* Retrieved from https://www.naeyc.org/academy/content/introduction-naeyc-accreditation-standards-and-criteria

National Association of School Psychologists. (2009). *Early childhood assessment (Position Statement).* Bethesda, MD: Author.

Organization for Economic Co-Operation and Development (n.d.). *Early childhood education and care.* Retrived from http://www.oecd.org/education/school/earlychildhoodeducationandcare.htm

Ramey, C. T., & Ramey, S. L. (1998). Prevention of intellectual disabilities: Early interventions to improve cognitive development. *Preventive Medicine, 27*(2), 224-232.

Ramey, C. T., & Ramey, S. L. (2004). Early learning and school readiness: Can early intervention make a difference? *Merrill-Palmer Quarterly, 50*, 471-491. doi:10.1353/mpq.2004.0034

Reynolds, C. R., & Kamphaus, R. W. (2003). *Handbook of psychological and educational assessment of children: Personality, behavior, and context.* New York, NY: Guilford Press.

Sheridan, S. M., Clarke, B. L., Knoche, L. L., & Pope-Edwards, C. (2006). The effects of Conjoint Behavioral Consultation in early childhood settings. *Early Education and Development, 17*, 593-617.

Shonkoff, J. P., & Marshall, P. C. (2000). The biology of developmental vulnerability. *Handbook of early childhood intervention, 2*, 35-53.

Shonkoff, J. P., Boyce, W. T., & McEwen, B. S. (2009). Neuroscience, molecular biology, and the childhood. *Journal of the American Medical Association, 301*(21), 2252-2259.

Treyvaud, K., Anderson, V. A., Howard, K., Bear, M., Hunt, R. W., Doyle, L. W., ... & Anderson, P. J. (2009). Parenting behavior is associated with the early neurobehavioral development of very preterm children. *Pediatrics, 123*(2), 555-561.

U.S. Department of Health and Human Services, Administration for Children and Families (January 2010). Head Start impact study. *Final report.* Washington, DC: Author.

U.S. General Accounting Office. (1997). *Head Start: Research provides little information on impact of current program* (GAO No. GAO/ HEHS-97-59). Washington, DC: Author.

Waanders, C., Mendez, J. L., & Downer, J. T. (2007). Parent characteristics, economic stress and neighborhood context as predictors of PI in preschool children's education. *Journal of School Psychology, 45*, 619–636. doi:10.1016/j.jsp.2007.07.003

Wakabayashi, T., & Beal, J. A. (2015). Assessing school readiness in early childhood: Historical analysis, current trends. In O. N. Saracho (Ed.), *Contemporary perspectives on research in assessment and evaluation in early childhood education* (pp. 69-91). Charlotte, NC: Information Age Publishing.

Wall, S., Litjens, I., & Taguma, M. (2015). *Early childhood education and care pedagogy review: England.* Paris: OECD

Wright, T. S. (2011). Countering the politic of class, race, gender, and geography in early childhood education. *Educational Policy, 25*(1), 240-261.

Reproduction of Chapter Thirteen: Interventions for Students from Low Resource Environments: The Abecedarian Approach

In *Essentials of Planning, Selecting, and Tailoring Interventions for Unique Learners*

We are reproducing this manuscript from the 2014 Wiley volume *Essentials of Planning, Selecting, and Tailoring Interventions for Unique Learners* by Mascolo, Alfonso, and Flanagan given its relevance to the special focus in this issue of PECPE. The authors of this chapter, Craig T. Ramey, Joseph J. Sparling, and Sharon L. Ramey are leading researchers, authors, and policy advocates for children living in poverty or otherwise low resource environments. Their work has been highlighted in leading journals, books, and policy statements for decades. They are especially known for their work in the development and implementation of the Abecedarian Project. It is an honor to reproduce their manuscript here as part of the special focus on Growing Up Poor: The Negative Sequelae on Child Development.

Thirteen

INTERVENTIONS FOR STUDENTS FROM LOW RESOURCE ENVIRONMENTS: THE ABECEDARIAN APPROACH

Craig T. Ramey
Joseph J. Sparling
Sharon L. Ramey

Children from poor and undereducated families are at high risk for developmental delay and lack of school readiness. This delay begins in early childhood and is routinely detectable by the second year of life (Martin, Ramey, & Ramey, 1990). Left unaddressed, the prognosis for normal development is bleak. To date we know of no school system in the United States that has reported data that show that these delays, frequently first detected in kindergarten, are routinely being eradicated in the early years of K–12 public education. By *routinely treatable*, we mean that the academic performance of such delayed development can be overcome so that high-risk children become indistinguishable in academic accomplishment from the typical U.S. student population. We hope that this bold statement will be contradicted by a slew of citations to the contrary. We have made this assertion in learned company before, however, without having our poor scholarship revealed.

If K–12 public education as practiced in the United States is

DON'T FORGET

Children from poor and undereducated families are at high risk for developmental delay and lack of school readiness. This delay begins in early childhood and is routinely detectable by the second year of life.

not equipped for this heavy lifting to counteract social and economic disadvantage, then what are the alternatives? Several possibilities come to mind:

1. Accept the status quo and live with the accompanying cascade of school failure, quitting school early, and the resulting sociodemographic and personal woes.
2. Pursue child-neglect legislation to prevent predicted harm through adoption.
3. Increase the school day and year so that children from low-resource families who are delayed get more effective and tailored instruction. This is often referred to as *tiered instruction* or *response-to-intervention*.
4. Pursue early childhood educational programs to prevent developmental delay by providing high-quality preschool programs that begin before delayed development occurs.

We and our colleagues have chosen to pursue the fourth option. Since 1972, we have been conducting a series of randomized controlled trials to test the proposition that systematic, individualized instruction beginning at birth can be a powerful tool to prevent intellectual delays and disabilities. In this chapter we present our educational model for the first three years of life and review our data relevant to the issue of the efficacy of preventive education.

The word *protocol* is used in this chapter to indicate that these Abecedarian concepts and procedures have been used as a tool in a series of scientific studies. The procedures collectively can be thought of as the "experimental treatment." In that sense, the *Abecedarian Protocol* (Table 13.1) is a set of standards, curriculum resources, and practices that were used in the interventions. *Abecedarian Approach* is the educational program and includes the four major *educational* elements of the intervention.

The major issue that drove the creation of the Abecedarian Project and its replication was whether the provision of theory-based, active learning delivered via early childhood education could produce preventive benefits in cognitive and social performance in children from highly impoverished, multi-risk families. Therefore, control groups of children who did not receive the Abecedarian Approach received the same levels of support as the educationally treated children for additional health care, free and unlimited nutritional supports, and active social work services to the families, as well as timely referrals when any problems were detected or suspected. Because the control groups received these multiple supports, the research findings provide a strong basis for concluding that it was the educational features of the Abecedarian Approach that produced the documented differences between the children in the experimental groups and the comparison groups to be summarized later in this chapter.

Table 13.1 Three Longitudinal Applications of the Abecedarian Protocol

	The Abecedarian Project	Project CARE	Infant Health & Development Program (IHDP)
Criteria for inclusion in the sample	Multicomponent socioeconomic risk (High Risk Score >11)[a]	Multicomponent socioeconomic risk (High Risk Score >11)	Low birthweight (< 2,500 g) and premature (< 37 weeks gestational age)
Duration of the child development center program	Age 6 weeks to age 5 years	Age 6 weeks to age 5 years	Birth to 3 years corrected age
Amount of child development center program offered	Full day,[b] 5 days/ week, 50 weeks/year	Full day, 5 days/ week, 50 weeks/ year	Full day, 5 days/week, 50 weeks/year
Visits in homes	As needed, for social support	Weekly educational visits (*LearningGames*®, 1979, 1984)	Weekly educational visits (*LearningGames*®, 1979, 1984, and *Partners for Learning*, 1984, 1995)
Health care	Onsite with nurses and MDs	Onsite with nurses and MDs	By family's own provider and with onsite pediatrician
Transportation to center	Provided by program	Provided by program	Provided by program
Parent-education group sessions	Several per year	Several per year	Every other month
Educational program	Abecedarian Approach	Abecedarian Approach	Abecedarian Approach

[a]The High-Risk Index for the Abecedarian Project and Project CARE.
[b]Children received approximately 8 hours/day, 5 days/week, and 50 weeks/year.

HISTORY OF IMPLEMENTING THE ABECEDARIAN APPROACH

The innovation of the Abecedarian Approach was to bring together for the first time the emerging scientific knowledge about how infants and young children learn and to incorporate these scientific principles into systematic playful learning activities and common caregiving routines. The steps in creating and implementing the Abecedarian Approach were sequential but overlapping. The following sections document a brief history of the Abecedarian Approach.

IDENTIFYING THE TARGET POPULATIONS TO RECEIVE THE PROGRAM

For the Abecedarian Project, and its first replication, *Project CARE*, a catchment area was identified and all providers of health care and social services to families were contacted about the project. Initially, the service providers identified women they thought were likely to be eligible based on their knowledge of the variables in the *High Risk Index* (see Table 13.2).

Table 13.2 High Risk Index for the Abecedarian Project and Project CARE

Mother's Educational Level (Highest Grade of School Completed)	Weights	Father's Educational Level (Highest Grade of School Completed)	Weights	Total Annual Family Income ($)	Weights
6th grade	8	6th grade	8	≤1,000	8
7th grade	7	7th grade	7	1,001–2,000	7
8th grade	6	8th grade	6	2,001–3,000	6
9th grade	3	9th grade	3	3,001–4,000	5
10th grade	2	10th grade	2	4,001–5,000	4
11th grade	1	11th grade	1	5,001–6,000	0
12th grade	0	12th grade	0		

Other Indications of High Risk and Point Values
Pts. (Weights)

3	Father absent from child's life for reasons other than health/death.
3	Absence of maternal adult relatives in local area (i.e., no parents, grandparents, or brothers or sisters of majority age).
3	Siblings of school age who were one or more grades behind age-appropriate grade, or who scored equivalently low on school-administered achievement tests.
3	Payments received from public assistance or welfare agencies within the past three years.
3	Record of father's work indicated unstable and unskilled or semiskilled labor.
3	Record of mother's or father's IQ score of 90 or below.
3	Records of one or more siblings with IQ scores of 90 or below.
3	Relevant social agencies in the community indicate that the family is in need of assistance currently.
1	One or more members of the family has sought mental health counseling or professional help in the past three years.
1	Special circumstances not included in any of the above that are likely contributors to cultural or social disadvantage.

Criterion for inclusion in high-risk sample is a score greater than or equal to 11.

Source: Ramey, C.T., & Smith, B. (1977).

Initial recruitment occurred when mothers were pregnant. The final screening to determine eligibility occurred after birth, with structured interviews, standardized assessments, and an intelligence test. Mothers with a High Risk Index score of 11 or higher were told about the project, the services that everyone would receive (nutritional, health, and social services), and the fact that half of them would be selected randomly (a process described as being like flipping a coin) to have their baby attend the child development center starting as early as 6 weeks of age and continuing until the child entered kindergarten.

CREATING THE CHILD DEVELOPMENT CENTER

The Abecedarian Project was implemented in a newly constructed *child development center*. The physical space for the child development program included rooms designed for infant care (until babies were walking, usually about 1 year of age) and large open spaces that were configured to serve separate groups of children of different preschool ages. The flexible and open space provided an easy way for the child development center staff and the leaders of the program to observe the teaching staff as they cared for children and implemented the curriculum. The classroom areas were approximately 1,000 square feet each, divided by low walls of bookcases or furniture. The physical space in each classroom was organized using the following principles (Harms & Cross, 1977), specifying that *nurturant care* environments for children should be:

- *Predictable* and promote self-help
- *Supportive* and facilitate social-emotional adjustment
- *Reflective* of the child's age, ability, and interests
- *Varied* in activities

We used child-sized furniture and stored toys and materials on low, open shelves to promote easy access by young children. Pictures, symbols, and/or word labels of the toys and materials designated the space these items occupied on a shelf or in an area. Through the use of pictorial labeling, even very young children were able to function somewhat independently in a print- and symbol-rich environment (see Rapid Reference 13.1 for principles of nurturant care environments).

We also felt that in a child development center, where children are part of a group, children might want to have privacy once in a while. In each classroom,

Rapid Reference 13.1 Nurturant Care Environments

Nurturant care environments for children should be:

- *Predictable* and promote self-help
- *Supportive* and facilitate social-emotional adjustment
- *Reflective* of the child's age, ability, and interests
- *Varied* in activities

DON'T FORGET
....
The use of pictorial labeling, even with very young children, can enable them to function somewhat independently in a print- and symbol-rich environment.

a slightly separated space was created for the child who wanted to get away from the group and be alone. In addition, each classroom had a warm, cozy area with a rug and pillows where children could sit or lie down. Children's work was displayed throughout the room, on cabinets, walls, doors, windows, and shelves, and changed frequently as children created new "products" reflecting their learning, interests, and creative expression. Each classroom had a dining space where teachers ate meals and snacks family-style with the children daily, as part of the structured program. Mealtimes were intentional learning periods with interesting table conversation to make mealtime a pleasant and educationally stimulating experience. Field trips brought variety into the program. Children explored and learned through trips to various community settings. Teachers typically planned with children, preparing them for the trip, and carried out systematic follow-up activities on returning to the center. The outdoor equipment for the Abecedarian Approach included a sand area, climbing equipment, and a paved track for wheeled toys. Outdoor activities were considered as educationally valuable as indoor experiences.

DON'T FORGET
....
Mealtimes with children can be used as intentional learning periods through the use of interesting table conversation. Such intentional conversation can make mealtime not only a pleasant experience, but an educationally stimulating one as well.

The nursery for children under 1 year of age was the only space that was not defined through the use of low bookcases and storage units. The nursery was a series of interconnected rooms. These provided differentiated space for sleeping and play.

≡ Rapid Reference 13.2 Organized Spaces

Organized spaces can help children:

- Feel comfortable.
- Find things easily.
- Use things frequently.
- Understand, in a very natural way, the similarities and differences among things that get stored together or not, and why.

We considered the organization of space and materials to be important mainly to help both the adults and children be comfortable, find things easily, and use them frequently (see Rapid Reference 13.2). We concluded that an organized child development center setting also would help children understand, in a very natural way, the similarities and differences among things that get stored together or not, and why.

The Abecedarian child development center teaching staff was comprised of a lead teacher and one or more assistant teachers in each child group. Our staff/child ratios ranged from 1:3 for infants and toddlers to 1:6 for 3-year-olds. We did not keep the ratios and age groups completely consistent at all times. Rather, the ratios shifted slightly from time to time as we sometimes staggered the dates at which individual children graduated from one group to the next.

A full-time *education director* based at the child development center provided administration and daily supervision of the child development teaching staff. The education director was an experienced, master's degree–professional who played a pivotal role in the child development center's delivery of effective services.

Perhaps because we were embarking on a concerted effort to create an innovative program that would be measured frequently, a strong team spirit grew within the staff. This was helped along by staff meetings and in-service training sessions. In these sessions the curriculum development staff met weekly or biweekly with the child development center staff, usually while the children were napping. (Volunteers from outside the child development center provided child coverage.) The meetings focused specifically on teaching, curriculum, and children's development. These sessions were substantive and strongly interactive. Administrative details were kept out of the meetings as much as possible.

HEALTH AND FAMILY SUPPORT SERVICES

The Abecedarian Approach focused strong attention on innovative early childhood education with the purpose of producing educational results. But it was not possible to set one's sights on child education without also paying attention to other areas of prime concern to vulnerable families: health, nutrition, social services, and transportation.

CAUTION

....

It is important to remember when planning early education interventions for children of vulnerable families that other variables, including family health, nutrition, need for social services, and transportation, may be equally important areas to attend to.

Health Services

The initial Abecedarian families were living in extreme economic poverty, and their health care was far from stable or of high quality. Therefore, we provided onsite child health care in the original Abecedarian Protocol and Project CARE. A *family nurse practitioner* (FNP) was onsite full-time and worked under the supervision of a pediatrician, who was on the faculty and a co-investigator. The FNP was a new health-profession role in the early 1970s and this proved to be an effective way to provide quality health care at a moderate cost in the child development center setting. (See, for example, Collier & Ramey, 1976, for a fuller description of the health-care issues.)

Nutrition

The research design of the Abecedarian Project specified that iron-fortified formula should be given to all children to reduce the possibility of early nutritional disparity between the educationally treated and untreated groups. (*Note*: Despite encouragement, no mothers elected to breastfeed their babies.) Families could pick up the free formula at the center. When the children were at the center, they received nutritious and attractive meals and snacks, always served with adults present as part of the educational protocol.

A registered dietitian planned the meals and snacks, which were prepared onsite in the Abecedarian Project, CARE, and four of the eight Infant Health and Development (IHDP) sites. The other four IHDP sites contracted food preparation from a local school or hospital foodservice.

Family Partnership and Family Support Social Services

Many of the low-income Abecedarian families had needs that resulted in seeking out the social services available in the community. Since the families were likely to continue to have these needs while enrolled in our program, we responded to these needs in the Abecedarian Approach through a combination of home visits, parent group meetings, and individual sessions with parents.

In the Abecedarian Approach, parent groups served several functions. They made it possible for parents to share information and concerns on childrearing. Being part of such a group allowed the parents to see that they were not alone in many of their concerns. Groups provided contacts among families that sometimes helped build social networks that were a source of support during the life of the program and sometimes lasted well beyond. Parent groups also provided information or access to resources in the community that may not have been otherwise available. For example, we often asked a person from the community to talk to the parent group about topics of interest or to describe programs that might be beneficial. See Rapid Reference 13.3 for a summary of the benefits of parent groups.

Home visiting was an integral part of the Abecedarian Project and its replications. Over time, our Abecedarian Approach used two different home visit strategies: (1) The original Abecedarian Project employed as-needed social work home visits made at least monthly, and (2) the CARE and IHDP Abecedarian replications employed regular parent–child educational home visits (with referrals for social work and health issues).

In the original Abecedarian Project, a staff member filled a supportive social work role, meeting with individual families (in both the experimental and the

≡ *Rapid Reference 13.3 Benefits of Parent Groups*

Providing a mechanism for parents to partake in parent groups (e.g., through access to community agencies that sponsor such groups) may prove important for intervention planning. Similar to the experiences of parents participating in the Abecedarian Project, such groups may:

- Enable parents to share information and concerns on childrearing.
- Help the parents to see that they are not alone in many of their concerns.
- Provide contacts among families that can help build social networks as a longtime source of support.
- Provide information regarding access to available community resources.

≡ *Rapid Reference 13.4 Planning Interventions*
for Vulnerable Families

Target goals when planning interventions for vulnerable families may include:

- Providing information on child development
- Providing health-care information and encouraging parents to use community resources as needed to maintain their children's health
- Providing emotional support to parents during stressful times
- Helping parents enhance their children's intellectual, physical, and social development
- Encouraging effective problem-solving
- Helping parents learn ways to positively interact with their children

control groups) in response to family needs or issues (see Rapid Reference 13.4 for points about planning interventions for vulnerable families). These were the issues that we found ourselves responding to:

- Health counseling and encouragement for healthy lifestyles
- Educational counseling and encouragement for mothers to continue their education
- Employment counseling and encouragement
- Lifestyle counseling and encouragement
- Crisis intervention
- Benefits counseling
- Transportation
- Cash assistance
- Neglect and abuse surveillance
- Home and neighborhood safety issues

In the CARE and IHDP replications, rather than making as-needed visits, teachers and/or visitors made weekly home visits on a regular basis and followed an agenda that was specifically focused on child and family education. In these educational visits, the home visitors were guided by the following goals:

- To provide information on child development
- To provide health-care information and encourage parents to use community resources as needed to maintain their children's health

- To provide emotional support to parents during stressful times
- To help parents enhance their children's intellectual, physical, and social development
- To encourage effective problem-solving
- To help parents with positive ways of interacting with their children

The Abecedarian Approach also included a toy-lending library as well as a book-lending library as a method of supplementing the educational resources in the home.

Transportation

Transportation was provided to and from the child development center on an as-needed basis to facilitate high attendance rates, which were in fact achieved. This was included because we felt that it otherwise would affect the participation rates of highly vulnerable families. Today it seems obvious that, to achieve the intended effect, a high level of participation in an intervention program is necessary. But the link between participation and outcome was not documented in the early 1970s. So, in the IHDP Abecedarian replication, we specifically studied child outcome as a function of participation in the first three years of the program.

DON'T FORGET

A high level of participation in an intervention program is necessary to achieve intended effects.

COMMITMENT TO HIGH QUALITY IN THE ABECEDARIAN APPROACH

In the Abecedarian Approach, there were four functional areas that were considered absolutely essential to help children grow and thrive. These areas were monitored through a variety of observational procedures, including video-taped time samples of classroom activities. These areas recently have been incorporated into an observational system known as the *Four Diamond Model of High Quality Early Care and Education* (Ramey, Ramey, & Sonnier-Netto, 2008, 2012; S. L. Ramey & Ramey, 2005; Table 13.3).

1. *Health and safety practices:* behaviors that seek to prevent all major problems and promote physical and mental health and safety, consistently implemented at all times.

Table 13.3 Four Diamonds Checklist

√ = YES
X = NO
N = NOT SCORED

Adult IDs	A_1	A_2	A_3	A_4

WARM AND RESPONSIVE CAREGIVING

				1. Adults* use children's names often with real warmth.
				2. Adults show joy, liking, and care for children.
				3. Adults often chat back and forth with children.
				4. Adults prompt children to explore and try new things.
				5. Adults answer children's questions and help them when needed.
				6. Adults care and teach about feelings and good ways to share them.
				7. Adults encourage and help children to play and get along with others.
				8. Adults watch children so they can adjust activities for each child.
				9. Adults make sure no child is teased or bullied. If so, they act quickly.
				10. For a child with special needs, adults learn ways to meet their needs.

LANGUAGE AND LEARNING ACTIVITIES

				1. Adults* help children be curious and eager about learning.
				2. Adults teach children lots of new words and phrases.
				3. Adults arrange toys and books so they are easy for children to use.
				4. Adults teach early literacy skills throughout the day.
				5. Adults teach early math skills throughout the day.
				6. Adults teach children a lot about "the big world."
				7. Adults use daily routines and in-between times to teach.
				8. Adults notice and show they care about what each child learns.
				9. Adults help children to plan and think about what they are learning.
				10. Adults keep records about each child's language and learning.

Time Observed _____ Date _____ Place _____

HEALTH AND SAFETY PRACTICES

1. Adults* always practice good hygiene.

2. Indoor and outdoor areas are safe and healthy.

3. Children and adults are physically active throughout the day.

4. Adults use safe practices when children behave badly.

5. Adults offer nap and quiet time throughout the day, but never harshly.

6. All adults look for and report possible abuse and neglect.

7. Adults use safe practices for napping, feeding, and going places.

8. Adults limit use of TV, video, and screen time.

9. Adults make sure almost all food and drinks are healthy.

10. Adults can use first aid and take care of problems.

FAMILY CONNECTIONS

1. Adults* ask parents to drop by, share ideas, and keep in touch.

2. Adults show warmth to parents and know their names.

3. Adults share with parents what children are learning and ways to practice.

4. Adults keep up-to-date about each child's family and home life.

5. Adults and parents meet often to talk about the child's growth.

6. Adults and parents talk about and try to fix problems.

7. Adults and parents help a child get ready for big changes.

8. Adults show caring and respect for all families.

9. Adults help parents learn about the rules in their setting.

10. Adults help parents protect children from harsh treatment and neglect.

Total √s

*Adult means any person who cares for a child on a regular basis.
© 2008, 2012 by Sharon Landesman Ramey, Craig T. Ramey, & Libbie Sonnier-Netto.

2. *Adult–child interactions:* behaviors that are frequent, warm, and responsive to the individual child.

3. *Language and learning activities:* adapted for the child's age and developmental level to maintain high interest and motivation.

4. *Caregiver–family relationships:* behaviors that are characterized as respectful, supportive, and informative; frequent communication between adults in the program and parents and other family members.

DON'T FORGET

Four areas that promote child development and are important to evaluate in intervention planning include:

1. The provision of consistent health and safety practices aimed at preventing health problems and promoting physical and mental health

2. Frequent, warm, and responsive adult–child interactions

3. Developmentally appropriate and interesting language and learning activities

4. Respectful and supportive caregiver–family or home–school relationships that are characterized by frequent communication

EDUCATION CURRICULUM

Children are learning all the time—put briefly, this was the explicit assumption based on research evidence and cognitive developmental theory. Therefore, the overall program and the educational curriculum were designed to be highly engaging, fun, and active—with learning occurring throughout the day in all activities (including daily caregiving, transitions, and physical play and exploration, as well as more structured learning activities). Activities included many adult–child individualized interactions as well as small-group activities, particularly as babies became older.

The systematic curriculum known as *LearningGames®* (Sparling & Lewis, 1979; Sparling and Lewis, 1984) was based on the identification of multiple types of learning processes in infants, toddlers, and young children—and was

DON'T FORGET

Intervention programs for children should be designed to be highly engaging, fun, and active—with learning occurring throughout the day and involved in a variety of activities (including daily caregiving, transitions, and physical play and exploration, as well as more structured learning activities).

paced to be appropriate for a child's developmental stage and to continuously provide challenges that were individualized for each child (Ramey, Yeates, & Short, 1984; Ramey, Breitmayer, Goldman, & Wakeley, 1996). The Abecedarian Approach strongly acknowledged the centrality of communication to the development of intelligence (McGinness & Ramey, 1981; Ramey, McGinness, Cross, Collier, & Barrie-Blackley, 1981). Thus, the planned "learning games" activities included many ways to use signs, symbols, sounds, words, sentences, stories, and interactive conversations—starting in the first year of life. Even conversational reading and play began in infancy with specially written picture/word books. Adults used varied, complex, and informative language throughout the day and the use of Standard English in the child development center was emphasized.

SUPERVISION FOR THE CHILD DEVELOPMENT PROGRAM

The Abecedarian Approach included supervision focused specifically on the main educational features of the program. The education director was the primary supervisor and mentor, supplemented occasionally by the curriculum development staff and the program leaders. In the Abecedarian Approach we recognized the central issues of the attitudes, knowledge, and skills of the adults who cared for and taught the children. Our goal was to have teachers/caregivers who would:

- Show positive attitudes about promoting the language and learning of children from birth.
- Believe that their own actions make a big difference and that their interactions in language and learning will have a major influence on how a child progresses.
- Know that very early learning opportunities and language stimulation are essential parts of their responsibility, and if they fulfill their responsibility they will help children get ready to succeed in school.
- Display frequent smiles, use positive words and tones of voices, display pleasant and encouraging actions toward all children, no matter what the time of day or how tired they may feel.

RATIONALE FOR THE EDUCATIONAL ELEMENTS OF THE ABECEDARIAN APPROACH

The Abecedarian Approach had an educational emphasis with multiple parts, including: (1) learning games, (2) conversational reading, (3) language priority, and (4) enriched caregiving. These were implemented in close coordination with a comprehensive curriculum framework described by Ramey et al. (1976). We provide a rationale for each of these elements in the following.

Learning Games

The Abecedarian Approach has an explicit developmental focus with game-like activities at its core. The central conceptual rationale for learning games derives from insights first presented by J. McVicker Hunt (1961) and elaborated educationally within Vygotskian theory (Vygotsky, 1978, 1986) and undergirded by the insights of Piaget and Inhelder (2000) and Bijou and Baer (1965), among others. In this view the fundamental ways in which a child's higher mental functions are formed are through mediated activities shared with an adult or more competent peer. Each of the learning game activities is one of these mediated activities. Vygotsky proposed that educational activities should be in a "Zone of Proximal Development"; that is, the activity should be one that the child can do with a little help. This concept is similar to what J. McVicker Hunt (1961) earlier called the *problem of the match*. So we consistently documented what the level of challenge to the child was and sought what was just the right amount of developmental challenge, at the right time. We believe that if instruction is too simple, not much new learning occurs; if it is too advanced, children are likely to experience frustration and failure and withdraw from the activity.

> **CAUTION**
> ....
> If instruction is too simple, not much new learning occurs; if it is too advanced, children are likely to experience frustration and failure and withdraw from the activity.

The curriculum development process for the LearningGames consisted of three steps: (1) Objectives were synthesized or selected, (2) curriculum products were developed, and (3) the curriculum products were evaluated. This work was mainly accomplished in a pilot phase of the Abecedarian Project with other children.

Our system for synthesizing curriculum goals has its origins in the theoretical position presented by Ralph Tyler (1950). Within this framework, curriculum objectives are seen as the product of the interaction of a number of sources or factors. Our formulation identifies the interacting sources as (1) consumer opinions, (2) developmental theory, (3) developmental facts, (4) adaptive sets, and (5) high-risk indicators.

The five sources from which the LearningGames were synthesized are pictured in Figure 13.1. The first source of curriculum goals is *consumer opinions*. Very

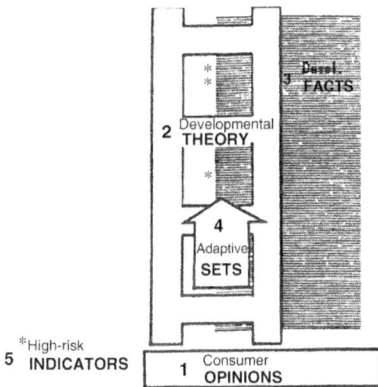

Figure 13.1. Five Sources for Synthesizing Curriculum Objectives

young children are, of course, the consumers of the infant curriculum. Through interviews, the hopes and aspirations parents have for their children were determined. Without this knowledge a project might proceed down a blind alley, producing a program that would in the end be rejected by the public it seeks to serve. It turns out that, in our experience, poor parents have remarkably similar hopes and dreams for their young children as do more affluent and educated parents. But they do tend to describe them using a somewhat different vocabulary.

DON'T FORGET

Poor parents have remarkably similar hopes and dreams for their young children as do more affluent and educated parents. But they tend to describe them using a somewhat different vocabulary.

The second source for deriving curriculum goals is *developmental theory*, largely that of Jean Piaget. The theory can be pictured as a ladder. On any rung of a ladder, one can look backward to see how the current status was arrived at or forward to see which steps are next.

The third source, *developmental facts*, acts as a background against which the developmental theory is viewed. Developmental facts provide a great amount of detail with which to supplement the theory. In this project, facts were gleaned from 30 sources, including Nancy Bayley, Charlotte Buhler, Arnold Gesell, Erik

Lenneberg, Dorothea McCarthy, Mary Margaret Shirley, and others. The facts were arranged in developmental sequence in four broad but overlapping developmental domains: language, motor, social/emotional, and cognitive/perceptive.

Of all the sources of educational objectives, the most important may be what we call *adaptive sets*. This is especially true for LearningGames because it was created with the explicit purpose of changing or enhancing the positive adaptive sets of the infant and young child. The child with strong adaptive sets has the tendency to move forward (for example, to explore rather than withdraw, to persist rather than give up easily). Therefore, adaptive sets can be thought of as that class of behaviors that predictably generate age-appropriate success. More simply, adaptive sets are "winning strategies" and are shown as an arrow moving up the ladder. The process of selecting statements of adaptive sets for this project, it should be clear, relies on professionally informed value judgments as well as relying on research findings. Because value judgments exist in *any* process of selection of educational objectives, LearningGames attempts to identify this potential bias by making it overt and subject to examination. For example, the following are among the statements of adaptive sets in the Abecedarian Approach. All of these behaviors can be thought of as being exhibited to an age-appropriate degree with extensive use desired by age 36 months:

1. Uses adults as resources
2. Controls his or her immediate environment
3. Uses both expressive and receptive language extensively
4. Detaches self from mothering adult and explores independently
5. Exhibits high-attention behavior
6. Responds frequently with positive approach to new object or person
7. Easily adapts to changes in environment
8. Executes multistep activities
9. Anticipates consequences
10. Explores extensively with the distance receptors (the eyes and ears)
11. Uses cooperative behavior
12. Uses basic sharing behavior (showing, giving, pointing)
13. Generates specific instances of a behavior by guidance of a general rule
14. Relates positively to the family

The final source of educational objectives was an awareness of *high-risk indicators* coupled with an effort to eliminate these in the child's repertoire. The indicators are seen in Figure 13.1 as asterisks or "warning signs" along the developmental continuum. To a substantial degree the high-risk indicator behaviors are the mirror image of the adaptive set behaviors. That is, the class of behaviors called high-risk indicators could be thought of as maladaptive sets, or perhaps "losing strategies." Because this curriculum was designed especially for children who are at a high risk of developmental delay and because research is beginning to document some of the behavioral deficits that high-risk children consistently develop, it is hoped that these deficits (here called high-risk indicators) can be anticipated through educational objectives that are basically preventive. A more detailed description of the development and evaluation of the LearningGames curriculum can be found in Ramey, Sparling, and Ramey (2012).

Conversational Reading

Conversational reading is the second aspect of the Abecedarian Approach. The conversational reading technique was partially developed and used in pre-publication form during our first two intervention studies (the Abecedarian Project and Project CARE). Its first published edition appeared in 1984, just in time for use in the IHDP eight-site Abecedarian replication. Significantly, conversational reading is modeled on the way parents and children typically read together rather than the way reading typically occurs in the classroom. Thus, our conversational reading approach goes back and forth, between adult and child, like a conversation. It would not be until the late 1980s that targeted experimental studies would support this interactive reading strategy, including the expanded technique developed and coined as "Dialogic reading" by Whitehurst (Whitehurst et al., 1988, 1994).

The key element of conversational reading was a questioning or prompting technique that was designed to elicit responses from children on three increasing levels of difficulty (see Rapid Reference 13.5). Some of these levels were easy enough for babies to participate in and some were challenging enough for older preschoolers. The technique invited children to see, show, and say something about the book and became known as the *3S Strategy*.

⬌ *Rapid Reference 13.5 Conversational Reading*

The key element of conversational reading is a questioning or prompting technique that is designed to elicit responses from children on three increasing levels of difficulty. The technique, known as the *3S Strategy*, invites children to see, show, and say something about the book being read.

CAUTION
....

Observational research has documented that high-resource families versus low-resource families show large and significant differences in adult language input and resultant child language, including child vocabulary and syntactic skill. As such, it is important for practitioners working with vulnerable families to integrate language activities wherever possible in intervention planning.

Language Priority

Giving priority to language means consistently weaving language stimulation into all parts of the day. This whole-day strategy was chosen because we thought language was likely to be the most important single pathway for the school success of children from poverty backgrounds, the group served exclusively in the first two Abecedarian studies. Since that time, careful observational research has documented that high-resource families versus low-resource families show large and significant differences in adult language input and resultant child language, including child vocabulary and syntactic skill (Ramey & Campbell, 1984; Hart & Risley, 1995; Huttenlocher, 1998).

Also since the 1970s when we developed our approach, other researchers have looked into homes and classrooms to discover and describe early language practices that are correlated with children's later success in school, especially in reading. Their analysis revealed three dimensions of children's experiences at home and in classrooms during the preschool and kindergarten years that are related to later literacy success: (1) exposure to varied vocabulary, (2) opportunities to be a part of conversations that use extended discourse, and (3) home and classroom environments that are cognitively and linguistically stimulating (Bradley et al., 1989; Dickinson & Tabors, 2001; Snow & Dickinson, 1991; see Rapid Reference 13.6). These documented practices have a lot in common with some of the assumptions we had made and the main language aspects featured in the Abecedarian Approach that we had adopted more than two decades earlier.

The language priority strategy we developed for the Abecedarian Project rested on several assumptions:

1. Gaining communicative competence is a primary goal.
2. Communicative competence is multifaceted, implying skills in at least three interrelated dimensions:
   a. Social (pragmatic) competence (language use).
   b. Representational competence (level of abstraction).
   c. Linguistic competence (language structure–syntax/semantics).

3. The child acquires effective communication skills mainly through exercising these skills with adults who are effective communicators and particularly in situations in which the child is able and motivated to engage intentionally in an interaction with the adult (McGinness & Ramey, 1981).

DON'T FORGET

Communicative competence is multifaceted, and includes skills in at least three interrelated dimensions:

1. Social (pragmatic) competence (language use)
2. Representational competence (level of abstraction)
3. Linguistic competence (language structure—syntax/semantics)

Enriched Caregiving

Certain actions and ways of interacting with children transcend the formal and explicit instructional curriculum. These actions comprise a *style* of education or intervention, and they are as important as other program elements. The Abecedarian Approach affirms that in the early years of life, education and caregiving cannot and should not be thought of as distinctly different activities.

The phrase *enriched caregiving* is intended to remind all of us (researchers, parents, caregivers, teachers, and program administrators) who care for an infant or young child that we can and should do several things at once. Care can meet the vital needs that support life and stimulate growth while also being responsive to the individual child's own preferences, abilities, and life situation. Further, care frequently can be enriched with educational content and individual flair. By highlighting the pivotal role of enriched caregiving in the education of young children, the Abecedarian Approach imbues all of the child's day with educational potential and meaning.

Enriched and responsive caregiving with protective and stable relationships is desirable and appropriate because it fits the contemporary notion of a humanistic

≡ Rapid Reference 13.6 Dimensions of Children's Home and Classroom Experiences

Three dimensions of children's experiences at home and in classrooms during the preschool and kindergarten years that have been found to relate to later literacy success include: (1) exposure to varied vocabulary, (2) opportunities to be a part of conversations that use extended discourse, and (3) home and classroom environments that are cognitively and linguistically stimulating.

436   ESSENTIALS OF INTERVENTIONS FOR UNIQUE LEARNERS

CAUTION

Facts About Stress, Cortisol, and Development:

1. Research has shown that brain development is negatively affected by higher levels of stress early in life.

2. Scientists have also found, studying both center-based and family-based child-care settings, that preschoolers have larger rises in cortisol (a stress-sensitive hormone) over the day if the site had lower quality of interaction between caregivers and children.

3. Other studies with young children have shown that levels of cortisol are related to memory, attention, and emotion in children.

approach to childrearing. But what is being learned about stress and brain development provides another strong reason for ensuring all children receive responsive care. Through animal research, it is known that brain development is negatively affected by higher levels of stress early in life (Sapolsky, 1996). Scientists have also found, studying both center-based and family-based child-care settings, that preschoolers have larger rises in cortisol (a stress-sensitive hormone) over the day if the site had lower quality of interaction between caregivers and children (Tout, de Haan, Kipp-Campbell, & Gunnar, 1998). Other studies with young children have shown that levels of cortisol are related to memory, attention, and emotion in children (Gunnar, 1998). Although we do not yet know conclusively whether early experiences of mild repeated neuroendocrine stress have long-term influences on the developing brain, researchers still conclude that "Taken together, these data strongly suggest that sensitive, responsive, secure caretaking plays an important role in buffering or blocking elevations in cortisol for infants and young children" (Gunnar, 1998, p. 210).

Responsive caregiving has continued to be documented and shown to relate to and stimulate basic areas of child development vital for school success. Using the longitudinal data set from the National Institute for Child Health and Human Development (NICHD) Study of Early Child Care and Youth Development in 10 sites, researchers asked how changes in the sensitivity of both mothers and caregivers from 6 months to 6 years relates to language and academic outcomes at the start of formal schooling. They found that sensitive and responsive caregiving is positively associated with better cognitive and language outcomes for children (Hirsh-Pasek & Burchinal, 2006). This longitudinal study also

DON'T FORGET

Sensitive and responsive caregiving is positively associated with better cognitive and language outcomes for children. As such, practitioners planning interventions for children of vulnerable families should assess caregiver styles and provide caregiving support, where feasible, via connecting families with community resources, providing parents with informational handouts, encouraging participation in parent groups, and so forth.

Table 13.4 Seven Essentials of Enhanced Caregiving

1. **Encourage**
   Encourage exploration with all the senses, in familiar and new places, with others and alone, safely and with joy.

2. **Mentor**
   Mentor in basic skills, showing the *what*s and *when*s, the *in*s and *out*s of how things and people work.

3. **Celebrate**
   Celebrate developmental advances, for learning new skills, little and big, and for becoming a unique individual.

4. **Rehearse**
   Rehearse and extend new skills, showing a baby how to practice again and again, in the same and different ways, with new people and new things.

5. **Protect**
   Protect from inappropriate disapproval, teasing, neglect, or punishment.

6. **Communicate**
   Communicate richly and responsively with sounds, songs, gestures, and words; bring the baby into the wonderful world of language and its many uses.

7. **Guide**
   Guide and limit behavior to keep the child safe and to teach what's acceptable, and what's not—the rules of being a cooperative, responsive, and caring person.

found a variety of positive effects at age 15 years for children who had been in higher-quality and more responsive care in the early years (Vandell, Belsky, Burchinal, Steinberg, & Vandergrift, 2010).

In the Abecedarian Approach we have summarized our enriched caregiving into seven classes of adult behavior, presented in Table 13.4 from Ramey and Ramey (1999).

SUMMARY OF FINDINGS

It is beyond the scope of this chapter to provide a detailed presentation of results that have been published in scientific journals. Rather we want to summarize two aspects of our findings to date: (1) the primary evidence relevant to consistency of findings across the three educational experiments and (2) the evidence concerning variations in curriculum participation patterns and child development outcomes.

Figure 13.2 displays the cognitive performance of the Abecedarian and CARE participants at 12, 24, and 36 months as a function of treatment and control groups. Analyses of demographic data showed high similarity of families and

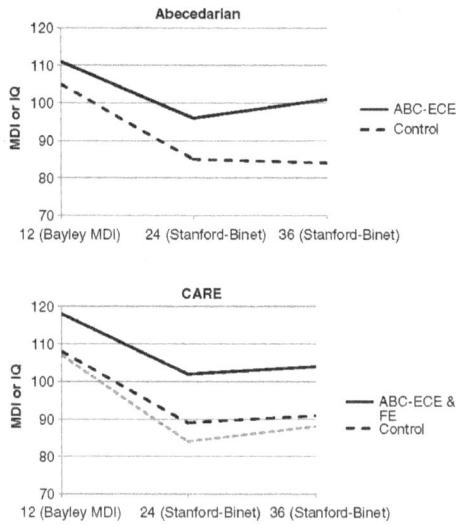

438   ESSENTIALS OF INTERVENTIONS FOR UNIQUE LEARNERS

Figure 13.2. Cognitive Performance of the Abecedarian and CARE Participants at 12, 24, and 36 Months

children at program entry (Burchinal, Campbell, Bryant, Wasik, & Ramey, 1997). On standardized measures of cognitive performance at 12 months there was a 6-point difference favoring the Abecedarian–Early Childhood Education (ECE) group and a 10-point benefit in the CARE–ECE group over controls. The difference between the Abecedarian–Family Education (FE) and control groups was not statistically significant at 12 months or any subsequent measurement occasion.

In both the Abecedarian and CARE experiments the cognitive differences between the Abecedarian Approach group and the control groups grew over time such that by 36 months the Stanford-Binet IQ difference was approximately 17 points for the Abecedarian–ECE group and approximately 13 points in project CARE (see Ramey, Yeates, Short, 1984; and Ramey, Bryant, Sparling, & Wasik, 1985 for a more detailed presentation of these findings for the two studies respectively).

Based on the results from these two experiments, my colleagues and I were offered the opportunity to test whether similar cognitive benefits might be obtained in a multisite randomized controlled trial. After much discussion about what was needed to move the field of early intervention forward, we decided to extend the test to a population that shared varying degrees of biological risk and varying degrees of socioeconomic risk. This was accomplished by competitively selecting eight sites to implement the first multisite controlled intervention trial for a randomly selected cohort of low-birthweight (LBW) (< 2,500 grams) and premature infants (< 37 weeks gestation). Because LBW and premature infants come from all socioeconomic strata, it afforded us the opportunity to examine the joint consequences of biological and social risk factors and to examine whether the Abecedarian Approach to Early Childhood Education would be differentially efficacious for particular subgroups of participating infants and their families. We separated the selection of LBW and premature infants into two groups: (1) children < 2,000 grams and (2) children between 2,001 and 2,500 grams. We selected $\frac{2}{3}$ from the lighter LBW group and $\frac{1}{3}$ from the heavier LBW group. A group at Stanford University was responsible for data collection and analyses and my colleagues and I, then at the University of North Carolina, Chapel Hill, assumed responsibility for oversight of the program implementation. The program, called the *Infant Health and Development Program* (IHDP), is described in detail in an article by Ramey et al. (1992). The measurement strategy for the cognitive performance for the children followed the form established in the Abecedarian and CARE projects to provide a direct comparison.

The cognitive performance data at 12, 24, and 36 months for the 2,001-to-2,500-gram group for each of the eight sites are presented in Figure 13.3.

At each of the eight sites the treatment and control groups were quite similar in Bayley Mental Development Index performance at 12 months but diverged in performance over the next two years. Analyses of each site indicated all eight sites differed significantly at 36 months with a mean difference slightly greater than 13 IQ points.

Figure 13.4 presents similar graphs for the < 2,000-gram infants. Individual comparisons revealed that 7 of the 8 comparisons were statistically significant at age 3 and at one site the scores at 36 months were almost identical. In addition, the magnitude of the differences was somewhat smaller at slightly greater than 6 IQ points when averaged across the eight sites. Because the Abecedarian and CARE samples were in the predicated direction at 36 months of age and significantly different across treatment and control comparisons, and because 15 of the 16 comparisons were as predicated in the IHDP, we can use the sign test to compare the results from the overall pattern of 17 positive signs for the treatment group

440 ESSENTIALS OF INTERVENTIONS FOR UNIQUE LEARNERS

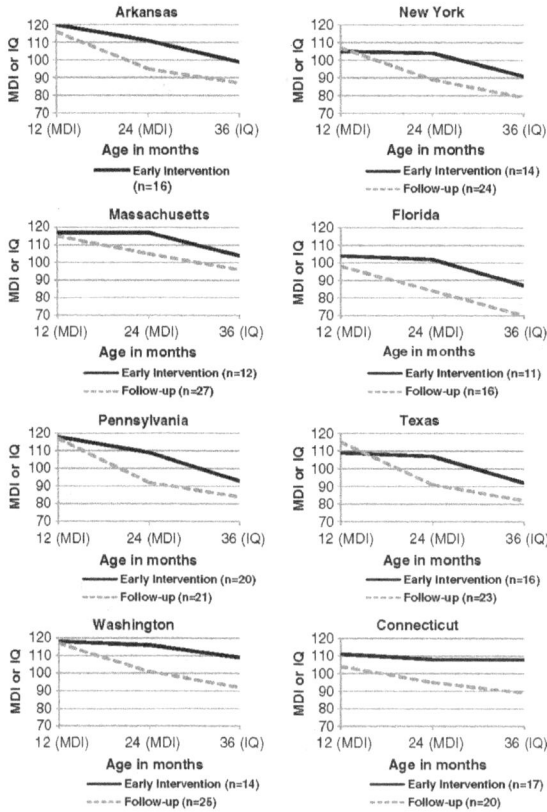

Figure 13.3. Cognitive Scores for Participants in the IHDP by Site for Infants 2,001–2,500 Grams at Birth

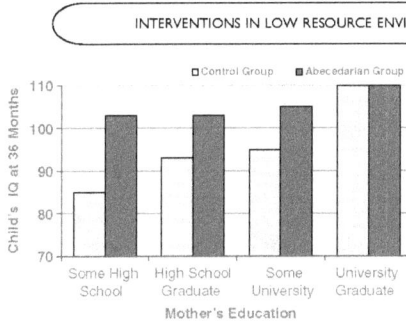

Figure 13.4. Child's Age-36-Months Stanford-Binet IQ by Mother's Education

over the comparison group (the tie score in the < 2,000-gram group in Massachusetts being eliminated); we calculate the likely result of this positive pattern as being $p < .001$ as a consequence of chance using the sign test (Siegel, 1956).

To address the issue of differential risk and differential response to intervention, we examined the Stanford-Binet IQ scores at 36 months as a function of the different educational backgrounds of the mothers of the low-birthweight infants. We grouped the educational backgrounds into four groups:

1. Less than high school graduate
2. High school graduate
3. Some university
4. University graduate

Results from this analysis are displayed in Figure 13.4.

The performance of the children in the control group shows a stair-step pattern with respect to maternal education. Children whose mothers had only some high school scored at approximately 85 on the Stanford-Binet IQ test at 36 months. Children whose mothers had a college degree scored at approximately 110. In the treatment group, all four of the maternal education groups had children who scored between 105 and 110. Thus, the effects of the Abecedarian Early Childhood Education program were to provide the greatest relative benefits to the children from the most disadvantaged families and to assist their development to the point that they were above national average and nearly comparable to that of the most educated group of families. In effect, the educational intervention nearly closed the cognitive achievement gap at age 3.

Further, the group that was most closely comparable to the original Abecedarian participants, the some-high-school group, showed a 20-point IQ advantage relative to the 17 points in the original Abecedarian experiment. From Figure 13.4 it is also clear that the Abecedarian Approach had neither a positive nor a negative impact on the IQ performance of children from college-educated families. Subsequent inquiry indicated that university-graduate parents of low-birthweight and premature infants used their resources to seek out developmental supports for their children that we were not able to improve upon with our treatment protocol.

HOW LEVELS OF PARTICIPATION ARE ASSOCIATED WITH CHILD OUTCOMES

In the Infant Health and Development Program, linking the process of early educational intervention to outcome provides important insights. The extensive data collected on implementation of the IHDP point to a variety of process factors that are predictive of a child's developmental progress in an early childhood intervention. The factors include, for example:

- Level of children's participation
- Amount of curriculum activities
- Rate of delivery of curriculum activities
- Degree of active experience for parents and children.

A major outcome demonstrated in the IHDP was a 9-point overall difference in IQ between the control and treatment groups at age 3. To explore a possible relationship between this 9-point difference in IQ and the level of children's participation in the intervention, we devised a participation index. This index was the sum of the number of contacts between each family and the intervention program, as measured by number of days a child attended the child development center, the number of home visits completed, and the number of group meetings parents attended.

Figure 13.5 shows the percentage of children who had borderline intellectual performance (IQ < 85) and impaired intellectual performance (IQ < 70) at age 3 according to three levels of program participation (low, medium, and high), compared to children in the control group.

The differences in the percentage of children at borderline or lower IQ at age 3 across the three levels of participation in the early educational intervention were dramatic, with an almost 9-fold reduction in impaired IQ performance associated with high participation relative to controls (Ramey et al., 1992).

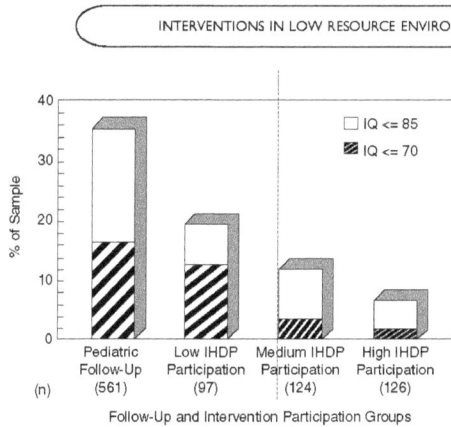

Figure 13.5. Percentage of Borderline (IQ < 85) and Impaired Intellectual Performance (IQ < 70) (IHDP, Infant Health and Development Program)

AMOUNT OF CURRICULUM ACTIVITIES

Another issue to be addressed is how much of the instructional curriculum each child receives when attending the center. This issue, of course, pertains only to the treated condition since the curriculum was not available to control group participants. Table 13.5 shows the mean IQ of children in the treatment group at age 36 months matched to birthweight and level of curriculum activities (low, medium, high) received in the child development center and at home.

The data show a positive relationship between mean IQ and level of curriculum activities for both of the low-birthweight groups. The higher the number of

Table 13.5 Mean IQ at Age 36 Months for Three Levels of Curriculum Activity Received by Children of Two Varying Birthweight Ranges (Infant Health and Development Program)

	Level of Curriculum Activity/Mean IQ		
	Low	Medium	High
Birthweight ≤ 2,000 g	82	95	97
Birthweight 2,001–2,500 g	92	98	100

Source: Sparling et al. (1991).

activities, the higher the child's IQ. Furthermore, among the children who received a low level of activities, those who had a lighter birthweight (< 2,000 g) had a 10-point lower IQ than did those who had a higher birthweight (2,001– 2,005 g) (Sparling et al., 1991).

Rate of Curriculum Delivery and Active Experience

In an independent analysis of the year-by-year levels of participation of individual children and families, Blair, Ramey, and Hardin (1995) discovered a clear association between participation levels and cognitive progress at ages 2 and 3. For each year from ages 1 to 3, the days attended by the child in the IHDP Abecedarian Approach Center, the number of home visits, and the number of parent meetings attended predicted cognitive advances or benefits, whereas the child's background characteristics such as maternal education and birthweight did not. That is, these high-risk children's early educational experiences exerted an effect that served to eliminate the usual negative toll of parent education, family's income, and other indicators of very low levels of home stimulation. This represents the strongest evidence to date about a dosage effect: The greater the level of exposure to high-quality learning opportunities, the more the child gained in terms of IQ points each year.

CONCLUSION

In this chapter we have presented the most detailed summary to date of the specific components of the Abecedarian Approach to developmental supports and early childhood education for the first three years of life. The Abecedarian components, in aggregate, have resulted in strong and consistent evidence that developmental delay can be prevented in high-risk children from low-resource families. This conclusion is buttressed by internal evidence that has linked the degree of curriculum implementation to cognitive developmental outcomes at 2 and 3 years of age. Further, the degree of implementation from year to year after the first year of life is directly related to the degree of developmental advance from year to year. We think that these regularities in the data are particularly noteworthy in light of the developmental services that both the control groups and the treated groups received, including nutritional supplements, family services, health care, and referral for developmental problems.

In our opinion, the issue of efficacy of early childhood education for high-risk children is settled. Yes, we can prevent a great deal of developmental delay. For us, the most pressing questions in early childhood education now become: (1) comparative efficacy of different early childhood programs, (2) differential response to treatment, (3) scale-up of effective programs, and (4) standards for programs aimed at preventing developmental delay. It feels good to move beyond the efficacy issue that dominated thinking about early childhood education for half a century.

REFERENCES

Bijou, S. W., & Baer, D. M. (1965). *Child development II: Universal stage of infancy.* New York, NY: Appleton-Century-Crofts.

Blair, C., Ramey, C. T., & Hardin, M. (1995). Early intervention for low birth weight premature infants: Participation and intellectual development. *American Journal on Mental Retardation, 99,* 542–554. PMID 7779349.

Bradley, R. H., Caldwell, B. M., Rock, S. L., Ramey, C. T., Barnard, K. E., Gray, A., . . . Johnson, D. L. (1989). Home environment and cognitive development in the first three years of life: A collaborative study involving six sites and three ethnic groups in North America. *Developmental Psychology, 25,* 217–235.

Burchinal, M. R., Campbell, F. A., Bryant, D. M., Wasik, B. H., & Ramey, C. T. (1997). Early intervention and mediating processes in cognitive performance of children of low-income African American families. *Child Development, 68,* 935–954.

Collier, A. M., & Ramey, C. T. (1976). The health of infants in day care. *Voice for Children, 9,* 7–11.

Dickinson, D. K., & Tabors, P. O. (Eds.). (2001). *Beginning literacy with language: Young children learning at home and school.* Baltimore, MD: Brookes.

Gunnar, M. (1998). Quality of early care and buffering of neuroendocrine stress reactions: Potential effects on the developing human brain. *Preventive Medicine, 27*(2), 208–211.

Harms, T., & Cross, L. (1977). *Environmental provisions in day care.* Unpublished manuscript.

Hart, B., & Risley, T. (1995). *Meaningful differences in the everyday experience of young American children.* Baltimore, MD: Brookes.

Hirsh-Pasek, K., & Burchinal, M. (2006). Mother and caregiver sensitivity over time: Predicting language and academic outcomes with variable- and person-centered approaches. *Merrill-Palmer Quarterly, 52*(3), 449–485.

Huttenlocher, J. (1998). Language input and language growth. *Preventive Medicine, 27,* 195–199.

Martin, S. L., Ramey, C. T., & Ramey, S. L. (1990). The prevention of intellectual impairment in children of impoverished families: Findings of a randomized trial of educational day care. *American Journal of Public Health, 80,* 844–847. PMID 2356909.

McGinness, G., & Ramey, C. T. (1981). Developing sociolinguistic competence in children. *Canadian Journal of Early Childhood Education, 1,* 22–43.

McVicker Hunt, J. (1961). *Intelligence and experience.* New York, NY: Ronald Press.

Piaget, J., & Inhelder, B. (2000). *The psychology of the child* (H. Weaver, Trans.). New York, NY: Basic Books.

Ramey, C. T., Breitmayer, B. J., Goldman, B. D., & Wakeley, A. (1996). Learning and cognition during infancy. In M. Hanson (Ed.), *Atypical infant development* (pp. 311–364). Austin, TX: Pro-Ed.

Ramey, C. T., Bryant, D. M., Sparling, J. J., & Wasik, B. H. (1985). Project CARE: A comparison of two early intervention strategies to prevent retarded development. *Topics in Early Childhood Special Education, 5,* 12–25.

Ramey, C. T., Bryant, D. M., Wasik, B. H., Sparling, J. J., Fendt, K. H., & LaVange, L. M. (1992). Infant Health and Development Program for low birth weight, premature infants: Program elements, family participation, and child intelligence. *Pediatrics, 89,* 454–465. PMID 1371341.

Ramey, C. T., & Campbell, F. A. (1984). Preventive education for high-risk children: Cognitive consequences of the Carolina Abecedarian Project. *American Journal of Mental Deficiency, 88,* 515–523. PMID 6731489.

Ramey, C. T., Collier, A. M., Sparling, J. J., Loda, R. A., Campbell, F. A., Ingram, D. L., & Finkelstein, N. W. (1976). The Carolina Abecedarian Project: A longitudinal and multi-disciplinary approach to the prevention of developmental retardation. In T. D. Tjossem (Ed.), *Intervention strategies for high risk infants and young children* (pp. 629–665). Baltimore, MD: University Park Press.

Ramey, C. T., McGinness, G., Cross, L., Collier, A., & Barrie-Blackley, S. (1981). The Abecedarian approach to social competence: Cognitive and linguistic intervention for disadvantaged preschoolers. In K. Borman (Ed.), *The social life of children in a changing society* (pp. 145–174). Hillsdale, NJ: Erlbaum Associates.

Ramey, C. T., & Ramey, S. L. (1999). *Right from birth: Building your child's foundation for life.* New York, NY: Goddard Press.

Ramey, S. L., & Ramey, C. T. (2005). How to create and sustain a high-quality workforce in childcare, early intervention, and school readiness programs. In M. Zaslow and I. Martinez-Beck (Eds.), *Critical issues in early childhood professional development.* Baltimore, MD: Paul H. Brookes, pp. 355–368.

Ramey, C. T., & Smith, B. (1977). Assessing the intellectual consequences of early intervention with high-risk infants. *American Journal of Mental Deficiency, 81,* 318–324.

Ramey, S. L., Ramey, C. T., & Sonnier-Netto, L. (2008, 2012). *The Four Diamonds Checklist.* Unpublished manuscript.

Ramey, C. T., Sparling, J. J., & Ramey, S. L. (2012). *Abecedarian: The ideas, the approach, and the findings.* Los Altos, CA: Sociometrics.

Ramey, C. T., Yeates, K. O., & Short, E. J. (1984). The plasticity of intellectual development: Insights from preventive intervention. *Child Development, 55,* 1913–1925. PMID 6510061.

Sapolsky, R. M. (1996). Why stress is bad for your brain. *Science, 273*(5726), 749–750.

Siegel, S. (1956). *Nonparametric statistics for the behavioral sciences.* New York, NY: McGraw-Hill.

Snow, C. E., & Dickinson, D. K. (1991). Skills that aren't basic in a new conception of literacy. In A. Purves & E. Jennings (Eds.), *Literate systems and individual lives: Perspectives on literacy and schooling* (pp. 179–192). Albany: State University of New York Press.

Sparling, J., & Lewis, I. (1979). *LearningGames® for the first three years: A guide to parent/child play.* New York, NY: Walker & Co.

Sparling, J., & Lewis, I. (1984). *LearningGames® for threes and fours: A guide to adult/child play.* New York, NY: Walker & Co.

Sparling, J., Lewis, I., Ramey, C. T., Wasik, B. H., Bryant, D. M., & LaVange, L. M. (1991). Partners: A curriculum to help premature, low-birth-weight infants get off to a good start. *Topics in Early Childhood Special Education, 11,* 36–55.

Tout, K., de Haan, M., Kipp-Campbell, E., & Gunnar, M. (1998). Social behavior correlates of adrenocortical activity in daycare: Gender differences and time-of-day effects. *Child Development, 69,* 1247–1262.

Tyler, R. W. (1950). *Basic principles of curriculum and instruction.* Chicago, IL: University of Chicago Press.

Vandell, D. L., Belsky, J., Burchinal, M., Steinberg, L., & Vandergrift, N. (2010). Do effects of early child care extend to age 15 years?: Results from the NICHD study of early child care and youth development. *Child Development, 81*(3), 737–756.

Vygotsky, L. S. (1978). *Mind in society: The development of higher psychological processes.* Cambridge, MA: Harvard University Press.

Vygotsky, L. S. (1986). *Thought and language.* Cambridge, MA: MIT Press.

Whitehurst, G. T., Epstein, J. N., Angell, A. C., Payne, A. C., Crone, D. A., & Fischel, J. E. (1994). Outcomes of an emergent literacy intervention in head start. *Journal of Educational Psychology, 86*, 542–555.

Whitehurst, G. J., Galco, F. L., Lonigan, C. J., Fischel, J. E., DeBarshe, B. D., Valdex-Menchaca, M. C., & Caufield, M. (1988). Accelerating language development through picture book reading, *Developmental Psychology, 24*, 552–559.

🐟 TEST YOURSELF 🐟

1. **How early is a developmental delay and lack of school readiness detectable in children who are at-risk because they are from poor and undereducated families?**

   a. The first year of life

   b. The second year of life

   c. The third year of life

   d. The fourth year of life

2. **In the Abecedarian longitudinal studies, the control groups of children who did not receive the Abecedarian Approach received the same levels of support as the educationally treated children for**

   a. Additional health care

   b. Free and unlimited nutritional supports

   c. Active social work services to the families

   d. Timely referrals when any problems were detected or suspected

   e. All of the above

   f. None of the above

3. **The Abecedarian Approach emphasizes four key educational elements. The key elements include all of the following except**

   a. Learning games

   b. Educational toys

   c. Conversational reading

   d. Language priority

   e. Enriched caregiving

4. **The conceptual rationale for the Abecedarian learning games derives from theoretical insights of**

   a. J. McVicker Hunt

   b. Lev Vygotsky

   c. Jean Piaget

   d. Bijou and Baer

   e. All of the above

   f. None of the above

(continued)

(*continued*)

5. *True or False?*: Since the time of the Abecedarian studies, careful observational research has documented that high-resource families versus low-resource families show large and significant differences in adult language input to children.

6. Dimensions of children's experiences at home and in classrooms during the preschool and kindergarten years that have been found to relate to later literacy success are

   a. Exposure to varied vocabulary

   b. Opportunities to be a part of conversations that use extended discourse

   c. Home and classroom environments that are cognitively and linguistically stimulating

   d. All of the above

   e. None of the above

7. The following element of the Abecedarian Approach has the special role of imbuing all of the child's day with educational potential and meaning:

   a. Learning games

   b. Conversational reading

   c. Language priority

   d. Enriched caregiving

8. *True or False?*: The National Institute for Child Health and Human Development (NICHD) Study of Early Child Care and Youth Development found no relationship between sensitive and responsive caregiving and better cognitive and language outcomes for children.

9. The Abecedarian study of low-birthweight infants found that the Abecedarian Approach provided the greatest relative benefits to the children of families with mothers whose educational level was

   a. Less than high school graduate

   b. High school graduate

   c. Some university

   d. University graduate

10. In the Abecedarian studies, which process factor(s) was(were) predictive of children's developmental progress in an early childhood intervention program?

    a. Level of children's participation

    b. Amount of curriculum activities

    c. Rate of delivery of curriculum activities

    d. Degree of active experience for parents and children

    e. All of the above

Answers: 1. b; 2. e; 3. b; 4. e; 5. True; 6. d; 7. d; 8. False; 9. a; 10. e

List of Contributors

Stephen J. Bagnato is a Developmental School Psychologist and Professor of Psychology and Pediatrics at the University of Pittsburgh, Schools of Education and Medicine. Dr. Bagnato holds joint appointments in Pediatrics and Clinical/Developmental Psychology and is Faculty Mentor for Early Childhood Partnerships at the University of Pittsburgh Office of Child Development. Dr. Bagnato is a core psychology interdisciplinary faculty member for the Leadership Education in Neuro-developmental Disabilities (LEND) Center at Children's Hospital of Pittsburgh of University of Pittsburgh Medical Center (UPMC), a United States Department of Health and Human Services (USDHHS), Maternal and Child Health Bureau LEND Institute.

Carol Barone-Martin is the Executive Director for Early Childhood Education at the Pittsburgh Public School District. She has been in this role for the past 13 years. Previous to this, Carol was the Executive Director for a non-profit child care and professional development organization, a child and adolescent therapist, a parent and community engagement specialist and a preschool teacher. Carol has her B.S. and M.S. in Child Development as well as a PA teaching certification and a supervisor certification in early childhood education. Carol lives in Pittsburgh, PA with her husband, two children and their dog.

Rachel E. Battaglia, Psy.D. is a graduate of Carlow University. Her residency was completed in Illinois with a focus on Clinical Child and Family Psychology with an emphasis on traumatic stress and family therapy. She completed her fellowship at Arkansas Children's Hospital with a focus on pediatric psychology. Rachel is currently a licensed psychologist in Pittsburgh, PA and works as a pediatric psychologist in a children's hospital. Her research interests include stress, psychosomatic symptoms of stress, and adjustment disorders related to chronic illness.

Nathan Beucke is an Associate Professor in the Department of Child Health. He is the Healthy Steps For Young Children physician champion in his academic general pediatrics office and an advocate for implementation of evidenced based screening tools in the clinical setting.

Evelyn Bilias-Lolis is an assistant professor for the Department of Psychological and Educational Consultation in the Graduate School of Education and Allied Professions (GSEAP) at Fairfield University. Dr. Bilias-Lolis has worked in adolescent mental health for over 10 years, helping to design numerous therapeutic programs for at-risk youth with a concentration in crisis counseling and intervention in the schools. Dr. Bilias-Lolis began her career serving as a school psychologist for a large urban high school while also serving as a behavioral consultant to local schools and specialized learning facilities. She later became the District Department Chair of Psychology and leader of the district Positive Behavioral Interventions & Supports (PBIS) Leadership Team. Dr. Bilias-Lolis holds an advanced training certificate in School Climate from the Connecticut State Department of Education. She has extensive experience in the systematic assessment of school climate. Her current research focuses on the application of positive psychology in the schools and the uncovering evidence-based positive psychological interventions that foster compassionate school practices. She teaches graduate courses in clinical and behavioral assessment of children, developmental psychology, behavioral statistics, psychopathology and classification, therapeutic treatment models, and psychotherapeutic techniques. Dr. Bilias-Lolis was awarded the Fairfield University Alph Sigma Nu Graduate Teacher of the Year in 2015.

Melissa A. Bray is a fellow of both the American Psychological Association and the American Psychological Society. Dr. Bray is an elected member of the Society for the Study of School Psychology. She is licensed as a psychologist in the State of Connecticut, holds national certification in school psychology, state certification in school psychology and licensure in speech language pathology. Since receiving her doctorate in 1997, she has published or has in press over 150 articles, chapters, and reviews in the professional literature, and has presented over 90 scholarly papers at national and international conferences. As co-principle investigator, she has secured over $ 1 1/2 million dollars in student training contracts. Of particular significance, Dr. Bray was the

2003 recipient of the prestigious American Psychological Association Division 16's Lightner Witmer Award, the Division's highest honor given to young scholars. Her research interests are in the area of interventions for communication disorders, classroom disruptive behavior, and physical health and wellness, especially asthma and cancer.

Sierra L. Brown, Ph.D., is currently a postdoctoral fellow and licensed psychologist in the Division of Autism Services at Penn State Hershey Medical Center. She currently provides clinical services and conducts research examining outcomes for adolescents and adults diagnosed with autism spectrum disorder (ASD). Her broad research interest includes children's social and emotional development.

Brandy L. Clarke is an assistant professor and licensed psychologist in the Department of Psychology at the Munroe-Meyer Institute (MMI) for Genetics and Rehabilitation at the University of Nebraska Medical Center (UNMC). She received her doctorate in school psychology in 2007 from the University of Nebraska-Lincoln. Clarke has co-authored numerous book chapters and peer-reviewed articles on the topics of early intervention, home-school partnerships, conjoint behavioral consultation, and integrated health care, and has also conducted local, national, and international trainings on such topics. As principal and co-principal investigator of several research studies in early intervention, Clarke has secured over $3,800,000 in grant funding. In addition, she serves on the Editorial Board for Psychology in the Schools and regularly serves as a guest reviewer for several other scientific journals in the field of early childhood and school psychology.

Natalie A. Drozda is a PhD student in the counselor education and supervision program at Duquesne University. She has been working as a graduate assistant for Dr. Waganesh A. Zeleke on numerous research projects on autism as well as mental health professional development in Africa. Her research interests include autism, trauma, post-traumatic growth, gender, and multicultural counseling.

Wendy Ell is a pediatric occupational therapist who has served as a coordinator of local and federal grant initiatives supporting young children's health. She has worked to advance evidence-based screening across both medical and educational early childhood settings.

Nick W. Gelbar is an assistant professor in Community Medicine and Health Care at the University of Connecticut Health Center and serves as the Research Director at the University Center for Excellence in Developmental Disabilities (UCEDD). Dr. Gelbar earned his PhD from the University of Connecticut in Educational Psychology with a concentration in School Psychology. He is also a licensed psychologist whose clinical and research work focus on adolescents with Autism Spectrum Disorder.

Scott L. Graves Jr., Ph.D., is an associate professor at Duquesne University. His interests can be broadly categorized as understanding protective factors that lead to appropriate development in early childhood. His research agenda is focused on identifying strengths in African American children that lead to positive social-emotional and academic outcomes.

Tammy L. Hughes, Ph.D. is professor and chair of the Department of Counseling, Psychology and Special Education at Duquesne University. She is the recipient of numerous awards for her teaching (*Trainers of School Psychologists; TSP*), research (Fr. Martin A. Hehir, Endowed Chair for Scholarly Excellence), service to the discipline (*American Psychological Association; APA, Pennsylvania Psychological Association; PPA*), and service to children (*National Association of School Psychologists; NASP*) among others. Active on the national level, she is the immediate past chair of APA's *Board of Educational Affairs* and is current serving as a *Council Representative* at APA as well as the co-chair of the Diversity Strand for the first national High School Summit for Teachers of Psychology in Secondary Schools (TOPSS). Dr. Hughes is an associate editor for *Journal of Early Childhood and Infant Psychology* and serves on the editorial boards of the *Journal of School Violence, International Journal of Offender Therapy and Comparative Criminology, International Journal of School & Educational Psychology* and the children's book series *Magination Press* where she provides notes to parents and caregivers on how to help young children overcome adversity. The author and co-author of over 100 scholarly publications, chapters, and books, her writing is in the area of understanding the relationship between emotional dysregulation and conduct problems in children. Dr. Hughes is a licensed psychologist and certified school psychologist. Her clinical experience includes assessment, counseling, and consultation services focusing on parent school interagency treatment planning and integrity monitoring. She is currently funded to work with families to help at-risk children stay in school; media interviews are available in print (CNN, ABA Journal) or on-line (Bullies, Victims and Bystanders: Tips for Teachers).

Tracy K. Larson is a nationally certified school psychologist and director of Early Childhood Partnerships at the University of Pittsburgh Office of Child Development. Ms. Larson has worked as a practitioner and researcher in early childhood psychology and education for over 20 years. Her interests include tiered prevention-intervention models to support high-risk young children and families. She is currently working on her Doctorate in Special Education and her dissertation will focus on educational services and supports for young children with emotional dysregulation and challenging behavior. Tracy lives in Pittsburgh, PA with her husband and three children.

Kara E. McGoey, Ph.D., is currently a professor of school psychology at Duquesne University where she teaches courses and conducts research on behavioral assessment and intervention, social-emotional development, and early childhood assessment and intervention.

Robin McNeal is a graduate student in the Applied Developmental Psychology program at the University of Pittsburgh and a trainee in the LEND (Leadership Education in Neurodevelopment Disabilities) center of Children's Hospital of Pittsburgh of UPMC. She is also a developmental healthcare consultant intern and research assistant for Early Childhood Partnerships at the University of Pittsburgh Office of Child Development.

She is interested in addressing behavioral needs in young children, and plans to pursue a career providing behavioral prevention and intervention services to high-risk children.

Maura A. Miglioretti is a doctoral student in the school psychology program at Duquesne University. She currently is working on her dissertation, which focuses on educational services for children with Pediatric Acute-Onset Neuropsychiatric Syndrome (PANS). She is a graduate assistant in the Department of Instructional Leadership in Education. She plans to become a nationally certified school psychologist and a licensed psychologist, and hopes to use her skills and education in community mental health and public policy administration.

Taylor Phillips is a graduate student in the school psychology program at Duquesne University in Pittsburgh, PA. She has been working as a graduate assistant for the Department of Counseling, Psychology and Special Education for the past year. Taylor has worked with Dr. Tammy L. Hughes on research projects that center on underrepresented populations, such as children of minority and low socioeconomic status, to identify risks associated with childhood trauma as well as how these risks are associated with aggression, delinquency, and incarceration. Taylor's professional practice goals surround providing specific intervention support to promote mental health to the most vulnerable populations. Taylor plans on becoming a nationally certified school psychologist and licensed psychologist.

Craig T. Ramey, Ph.D., is the originator and founding principal investigator for the Abecedarian Project, Project CARE, and the Infant Health and Development Program. He currently holds the positions of Professor and Distinguished Research Scholar of Hu¬man Development at the Virginia Tech Carilion Research Insti¬tute; Professor of Psychology, Neuroscience, and Human Development at Virginia Tech; Professor of Pediatrics at the Virginia Tech Carilion School of Medicine; and Chief Science Officer for Human Development, City of Roanoke, Virginia . Craig Ramey is a lifespan developmental psychologist.

Sharon Landesman Ramey, Ph.D., formerly served as Director of the Frank Porter Graham Child Development Institute and joined the large, multidisciplinary research team engaged in the studies presented in this article. She is now a Professor and Distin¬guished Research Scholar at the Virginia Tech Carilion Re¬search Institute; Professor of Psychology, Neuroscience, and Human Development at Virginia Tech; Professor of Psychiatry and Behavioral Medicine at the Virginia Tech Carilion School of Medicine; and Chief Science Officer for Human Development, City of Roanoke, Virginia.

Robert A. Reed (Bob) is a professor of psychology and counseling at Carlow University where he teaches in the graduate school. In addition to being an academic Bob has a long history of clinical work specializing with families and children.

Kristin M. Rispoli, Ph.D. is an assistant professor in the School Psychology program at Michigan State University, a licensed psychologist, and a nationally certified school psychologist. Dr. Rispoli has over 10 years' experience conducting assessment, intervention, and consultation services for children with behavioral and developmental disabilities. Her scholarly interests include the efficacy and importance of supporting child social-emotional competence and family-school partnerships in children from pre-kindergarten through post-secondary transition. Dr. Rispoli's current research is focused on characterizing and fostering effective practices to involve parents in education and treatment for children with or at-risk for disabilities, and developing efficacious interventions to support social-emotional competence in young children with autism spectrum disorder (ASD). She has obtained external funding to support her work through organizations including the Society for the Study of School Psychology and the Organization for Autism Research.

James B. Schreiber, Ph.D. is a professor of epidemiology and statistics in the School of Nursing at Duquesne University. He received his Ph.D. from Indiana University Bloomington in 2000. He has published over 60 articles, reviews, and book chapters along with over 120 national and international conference presentations. Previously, he was a high school mathematics teacher and department chair, a Professor of Education, and Associate Dean for Teacher Education.

Joseph J. Sparling, Ph.D., is currently a Senior Scientist Emer¬itus at the Frank Porter Graham Child Development Institute, University of North Carolina at Chapel Hill, and Honorary Professorial Fellow, Graduate School of Education, University of Melbourne, Australia. He is an early childhood educator and one of the original authors of the LearningGames® and Partners for Learning curricula used in all of the Abecedarian Approach research projects.

Melissa Stormont is a professor in the Department of Special Education. She has published extensively in the areas of early childhood and prevention science; specifically she has published over one hundred peer-reviewed articles, books, and book chapters. She is involved in numerous federal and local grants to support the use of evidence-based practices in supporting social, emotional, and mental health development in children.

Amy E. Tiberi is a graduate student in the school psychology program at Duquesne University in Pittsburgh, PA. She has been working as a graduate assistant for the Department of Counseling, Psychology and Special Education for the past 3 years. Amy has worked with Dr. Tammy L. Hughes on research projects related to educational disparities and access to mental health services for youth, advocacy, and consultative practices for adjudicated students that are involved in the juvenile justice system. Amy is currently studying school-based policies for LGBTQ+ youth for her dissertation. She plans on becoming a nationally certified school psychologist and licensed psychologist, and hopes to work in academia.

Laine Young-Walker is an associate professor in the Department of Psychiatry. She obtained federal and local grants to establish programs utilizing evidence-based practices in supporting the social and emotional well-being of young children.

Waganesh A. Zeleke is an Assistant Professor in the Department of Counseling, Psychology, and Special Education at Duquesne University where she teach different graduate level courses in the master's and doctoral program. She is a licensed clinical mental health counselor and national certified counselor. Her clinical experience include counseling and consultation services focusing on autism spectrum disorder (ASD), child-family relationship development, post traumatic stress disorder, parenting consultation, intercultural adoption, attachment, mental health issues among immigrant population, and childhood mental disorders in US and Africa. Dr. Zeleke has co-authored and authored publications in topics related to clinical interviewing, ASD, and family relational development, mental healthcare access, and utilization of children with ASDs. Dr. Zeleke's research focus primarily on two lines of inquire: 1) Examining mechanisms that underlie the mental health development and psychological adjustment of African and African Diaspora communities who primarily experience migration and or international adoption. 2) Research leading to a better understanding and treatment methods of individual with ASD in Africa and USA.

GENERAL ARTICLE

Reliability of the Classroom Assessment Scoring System (CLASS K-3) in Primary Classrooms

Molly S. Kaufman and James C. DiPerna

Abstract

The purpose of the current study was to evaluate the inter-rater reliability, internal consistency, and long-term stability of scores from the Classroom Assessment Scoring System, Kindergarten-Third Grade (CLASS K-3; Pianta, La Paro, & Hamre, 2008). Paired observations ($N = 157$) were conducted in first- and second-grade classrooms. When inter-rater reliability was examined using less stringent indices (e.g., percent-within-one, intraclass correlation) results consistently exceeded minimum thresholds for agreement. However, when more stringent indices (e.g., exact agreement, Cohen's kappa, linearly weighted kappa) were used, results were lower. Internal consistency coefficients were high across domains, and long-term stability coefficients were low to moderate. Overall, results were similar to those from previous reliability studies of CLASS at other grade levels.

Key Words: Classroom Assessment Scoring System, CLASS K-3, reliability, early childhood

Classrooms environments are complex systems, and as a result, they have been difficult to assess. The Classroom Assessment Scoring System (CLASS; Pianta, La Paro, & Hamre, 2008) was developed to address this challenge by providing both practitioners and researchers an observation-based assessment of the classroom environment. Its aim is to measure to what extent teachers are supporting students' academic and social development (Hamre, Goffin, & Kraft-Sayre, 2009). Although studies of the CLASS have demonstrated some evidence to support the reliability and validity of its scores, few independent evaluations of the elementary version of the CLASS, CLASS K-3, have been completed to date. Given its growing use in primary classrooms, examining the reliability and validity of CLASS K-3 scores is essential to ensure that they are used appropriately. To date, there has been only one independent study of CLASS score reliability (Sandilos & DiPerna, 2011); however, this study examined reliability of the pre-kindergarten version of the CLASS. As such, the purpose of the current study was to examine reliability of scores from the elementary version of the CLASS in first and second grade classrooms.

CLASS K-3

Although environmental factors have been assessed by a number of early childhood rating systems, recent research has indicated that environmental factors (e.g., length of the school day, number of books in a classroom, teacher-student ratios) are not sufficient indicators of classroom quality (Pianta, Downer, & Hamre, 2016). Unlike these earlier measures, the CLASS focuses on the quality of relationships within the classroom (Hamre et al., 2009). More specifically, the CLASS assesses classrooms along three broad domains (emotional support, classroom organization, and instructional support), and each domain is comprised of several dimensions (e.g., positive climate, behavior management, and quality of feedback). Collectively, these domains and dimensions measure the extent to which teachers are supporting students' academic and social development (Hamre et al., 2009).

According to Pianta et al. (2008) scores from the CLASS can be used for a number of purposes including research, school accountability efforts, program planning and evaluation, and professional development. At an individual level, the CLASS can be used to provide current and preservice teachers direct feedback about their classroom practices. Furthermore, CLASS K-3 data can be used in conjunction with other CLASS resources, such as the MyTeachingPartner (Hadden & Pianta, 2006), to offer on-going and individualized feedback. At a systems-level, the CLASS can be used to examine districtwide strengths and weaknesses of classroom factors that may be targeted for intervention. Stuhlman, Hamre, Downer, and Pianta (n.d.) also suggested that CLASS observational data be used descriptively to highlight areas of relative strength and weakness. They caution, however, that there is little data to suggest using cut-off scores to determine proficiency. Despite this recommendation, the CLASS has been used in this way, for example, within the Head Start Designation and Renewal System (Derrick-Mills et al., 2016).

Since its release, the CLASS has been widely adopted for use in early childhood classrooms (Hamre et al., 2009). In addition, the CLASS has been used for a number of early childhood program evaluation efforts (e.g., Derrick-Mills et al., 2016). Given the growing popularity and use of the CLASS for a variety of purposes, it is important to consider the reliability evidence behind CLASS scores.

Reliability Evidence for CLASS Scores

As reported in the technical manual (Pianta et al., 2008), CLASS scores have demonstrated high inter-rater agreement (.79-.97), internal consistency (.71-.91), and short-term stability (.73-.85). Additionally, domain scores have demonstrated moderate stability (.25-.64) between the fall and spring of one academic year. Although these data are reported in the CLASS K-3 manual, with the exception of internal consistency, all indices were calculated using data collected with the CLASS pre-K. This gap is notable in that evidence from the pre-K version may not generalize to the K-3 version given differences between preschool and early elementary classrooms. In addition, the long-term stability (i.e., across more than one academic year) of CLASS K-3 scores has not been examined to date, and such evidence is important if these scores are to be used to provide formative feedback to classroom teachers over time.

A number of studies featuring the CLASS K-3 report reliability estimates based on data from observer training sessions (e.g., Cadima, Leal, & Burchinal, 2010; Curby, Rimm-Kaufman, & Ponitz, 2009; Plank & Condliffe, 2013), which feature observations of pre-recorded videos. These training observations are completed as part of an extensive (two-day) training protocol for observers to become certified to conduct field-based CLASS observations (Hamre & Pianta, 2005). For individuals to become certified observers, they must meet a threshold of at least 80% reliability when observing the CLASS training videos. A few studies have reported ancillary analyses of reliability data from live observations, however, these analyses featured less stringent estimates of reliability (e.g., Brown, Jones, LaRusso, & Aber, 2010; Sandilos, 2012).

In an independent study of the inter-rater reliability of the CLASS pre-K, Sandilos and DiPerna (2011) examined reliability of CLASS observations in real-time. Although the study featured a small and homogeneous sample of preschool classrooms, their initial results were consistent with the inter-rater reliability evidence reported in the manual for the CLASS Pre-K. When applying more stringent methods to their data (e.g., kappa), however, Sandilos and DiPerna found lower estimates of reliability.

Rationale

The growing use of the CLASS K-3 necessitates that its scores demonstrate adequate psychometric properties; however, reliability evidence to date has been examined primarily with the pre-K version of the CLASS and is limited to observations of classroom videos. As Sandilos and DiPerna (2011) noted, reliability estimates based on observations of videos may not accurately reflect reliability of scores based on real-time observations in classroom settings. Similarly, reliability evidence for the CLASS pre-K may not accurately reflect reliability of scores from the CLASS K-3 version. As such, the current study investigated the reliability of CLASS K-3 utilizing in-vivo observations in first and second grade classrooms.

This study is the first independent evaluation of the reliability of CLASS K-3 scores, and it replicates the methodology of Sandilos and DiPerna (2011) which examined multiple reliability indices for the CLASS pre-K. Replication studies, particularly those conducted by independent evaluators, are significantly underrepresented in educational literature despite representing a very important contribution to the knowledge base (Makel & Plucker, 2014). Based on previous studies with the CLASS pre-K (Pianta et al., 2008; Sandilos & DiPerna, 2011), we hypothesized that CLASS K-3 scores demonstrate high internal consistency and inter-rater reliability when using less-stringent reliability indices. We expected lower inter-rater reliability estimates, however, when using more conservative indices of agreement. In addition, we hypothesized that CLASS K-3 domain scores demonstrate low to moderate long-term stability.

Method

Participants

Observations were drawn from 50 first and second grade classrooms in one urban and one rural school district. The student population in the rural district was fairly homogeneous with regard to student race (91% Caucasian); whereas the urban district was more diverse (45% Caucasian, 32% African-American, and 12% Hispanic). The average class size was 19 students (SD = 3.32). The majority of classrooms (72%) had one teacher present during the observations, while the remaining 28% of classrooms also had at least one support staff present during observations. First grade teachers were exclusively female, almost entirely Caucasian (98.2%), and had an average of approximately 17 years of teaching experience. Second grade teachers were primarily female (79.7%) and Caucasian (97.5%) with an average of 16.58 years of experience.

Measures

The CLASS K-3 is designed to measure the quality of teacher-student interactions and the way in which teachers implement resources (Hamre et al., 2009). Specifically, it examines interactions based on three broad domains: emotional support, classroom organization, and instructional support. The emotional support domain assesses the dimensions of positive climate, negative climate, teacher sensitivity, and regard for student perspectives. The classroom organization domain assesses the dimensions of behavior management, productivity, and instructional learning formats. The instructional support domain assesses the dimensions of concept development, quality feedback, and language modeling. Scoring for each dimension is based on a 7-point scale. A score of 1-2 is in the low range, a score of 3-5 is in the middle range, and a score of 6-7 is in the high range. Scores are assigned to each dimension after a trained rater completes a series of one to four observation cycles (Hamre et al., 2009).

Procedure

Data were drawn from an ongoing multiyear study examining the efficacy of a class-wide social skills program. As part of that study, baseline, post-intervention, and follow-up measures of instructional environments were collected using the CLASS K-3. These scores demonstrated no significant relationship with the intervention; thus, all paired observations were used in the current study. Data were collected from 50 classrooms over a 3-year period yielding 157-paired observations. Written consent was obtained from teachers in participating classrooms.

In order to collect data, 15 research staff, two male and 13 female, served as classroom raters. All staff had at least a bachelor's degree in psychology, education, or a related field. Staff were trained by a certified CLASS instructor and obtained mastery (at least 80%) in observational coding. This training protocol was consistent with the preparation described by the test developers (Hamre et al.,

2009). In addition, two observation cycles were completed for each classroom in the current study. Each cycle consisted of 20 minutes of observation and 10 minutes of assigning ratings, thus observers spent 1-hour total engaged in each observation. Two cycles of CLASS observations have been utilized frequently in previous research and evaluation efforts (e.g., Derrick-Mills et al., 2016; Sandilos & DiPerna, 2011), and data reported in the CLASS manual indicate strong correlations among domain and dimension scores obtained from two cycles and four cycles of observation (Pianta et al., 2008). All observations were paired, meaning two staff members observed classrooms simultaneously.

Design and Data Analysis

Consistent with the work of Sandilos and DiPerna (2011), reliability was examined based upon a number of different indices, including PWO, exact agreement, intraclass correlations (ICC), Cohen's kappa, linearly weighted kappa, internal consistency, and score stability. In the CLASS Technical Manual, Pianta et al. (2008) used an 80% minimum reliability threshold for PWO, and this criterion was applied to data in the current study as well. Specifically, scores are considered to be in agreement if they are within 1 point of each other. In order to evaluate the precision of scores, percentage of items demonstrating exact agreement also was examined. ICC represent the strength of the relationship between two or more ratings of the same target (Howell, 2010), thus it serves as a general measure of agreement. These indices are limited, however, in that they fail to account for agreement that may occur due to chance. In order to account for chance agreement, Cohen's kappa and linearly weighted kappa also were calculated.

Internal consistency reflects whether dimensions within the same domain measure the same construct and thus, produce similar scores. Cronbach's alpha was computed as an estimation of internal consistency for each domain. Score stability, for the purposes of the current study, was examined over a period of approximately

10 months. Stability was computed using ICCs to examine the extent to which scores are similar across time.

Results

Descriptive Analyses & Assumptions

Analyses were conducted using SPSS version 22 and R Studio version 0.98.1091. Table 1 contains means, standard deviations, skew, and kurtosis values for all dimensions. Skew and kurtosis values of +/– 1.96 are generally considered to be within the normal range (Field, 2013). All values fell within this range with the exception of the dimension of negative climate (skew = 2.70; kurtosis = 7.65). Q-Q plots were examined to approximate normality as well. Again, all data appeared to be normally distributed except for negative climate. The non-normal distribution of scores for negative climate clustered around a score of 1, which is consistent with what has been reported elsewhere (e.g., Early Childhood Learning & Knowledge Center, 2014; Pianta et al., 2008; Sandilos, 2012).

Primary Analyses

Inter-rater agreement indices are reported in Table 2. Values for PWO agreement were calculated for each 20-minute observation cycle as each rating was assigned independently at the end of the observation period. Across all dimensions, domains, and cycles, values were above 90% with the exception of productivity (78% for cycle 2). Values for exact agreement varied within each cycle, ranging from 33-84%. The smallest domain values were observed for emotional support. For dimensions, the majority of values fell in the 59-67% range, except for negative climate, which had scores ranging from 83-84%. ICCs were calculated independently for cycle 1 and 2, and values ranged from .80 to .93. Cohen's kappa yielded the lowest agreement estimates for domains (.28-.39), though values were higher for dimensions (.58-.71). Linearly

Table 1:
Means, Standard Deviations, Skew, and Kurtosis for CLASS K-3 Scores

Domain/ dimension	Cycle 1			Cycle 2		
	M (SD)	Skew	Kurtosis	M (SD)	Skew	Kurtosis
Emotional support	3.88 (0.63)	-0.50	-0.19	4.04 (0.63)	-0.33	-0.13
Positive climate	5.14 (1.28)	-0.29	-0.66	5.17 (1.25)	-0.21	-0.66
Negative climate	1.31 (0.55)	2.20	3.80	1.42 (0.54)	1.83	2.98
Teacher sensitivity	4.64 (1.14)	-0.31	-0.71	4.69 (1.16)	-0.13	-0.46
Regard for student perspectives	3.83 (1.16)	-0.16	-0.32	3.63 (1.16)	0.42	-0.36
Classroom organization	5.38 (0.90)	-0.89	0.47	5.16 (0.97)	-1.03	1.03
Behavior management	5.83 (1.17)	-0.90	0.48	5.62 (1.30)	-1.12	1.35
Productivity	5.61 (1.15)	-0.72	0.08	5.42 (1.26)	-0.63	-0.14
Instructional learning formats	4.70 (1.00)	-0.15	-0.05	4.45 (1.12)	-0.26	-0.20
Instructional support	2.52 (1.04)	0.47	-0.60	2.35 (1.04)	0.84	0.36
Concept development	2.55 (1.18)	0.30	-0.89	2.37 (1.14)	0.58	-0.44
Quality of feedback	2.61 (1.26)	0.48	-0.62	2.43 (1.30)	0.90	0.27
Language modeling	2.41 (1.12)	0.70	0.08	2.25 (1.15)	0.67	-0.31

Note. Maximum range of domain and dimension scores is 1 – 7.

weighted kappa estimates were highest for domains (.67-.69) and lower across all dimensions (.43-.55).

Internal consistency and long-term stability also were examined to offer insight regarding other aspects of reliability. Internal consistency of domains were as follows: emotional support (.85), classroom organization (.88), and instructional support (.93). Long-term stability (Table 3) was examined using two ratings of the same classroom that were collected 10 months apart on average (across 2 consecutive academic years). Coefficients varied across all domains and dimensions (.21-.71). The least stable dimensions were concept development, teacher sensitivity, productivity, and language modeling. The most stable dimensions were positive climate, behavior management, instructional learning formats, and quality feedback. At the domain level, emotional support and classroom organization were the most stable and instructional support was the least stable.

Table 2:
Inter-Rater Agreement Indices of Reliability for CLASS K-3 Scores

Domain/ dimension	ICC		Percent agreement				Kappa	
			PWO		Exact		Cohen's	Weighted
	Cycle 1	Cycle 2	Cycle 1	Cycle 2	Cycle 1	Cycle 2	Combined cycles	Combined cycles
Emotional support	.94*	.90*	99	96	33	37	.28	.67
Positive climate	.89*	.93*	93	97	63	67	.70	.55
Negative climate	.90*	.81*	99	97	84	83	.66	.55
Teacher sensitivity	.89*	.82*	96	91	60	58	.61	.45
Regard for student perspectives	.91*	.87*	97	96	63	55	.65	.47
Classroom organization	.92*	.93*	96	95	44	42	.36	.69
Behavior management	.87*	.91*	95	94	59	67	.67	.51
Productivity	.92*	.92*	97	78	67	67	.71	.55
Instructional learning formats	.80*	.87*	95	96	63	55	.58	.43
Instructional support	.92*	.90*	96	91	44	46	.39	.69
Concept development	.90*	.87*	96	94	60	78	.66	.51
Quality of feedback	.91*	.83*	95	91	60	56	.64	.46
Language modeling	.88*	.93*	96	98	63	71	.69	.55

*Note. Percent-within-one (PWO) is the percent of scores that are within 1 point of each other. *p<.01.*

Discussion

The purpose of this study was to examine reliability of CLASS K-3 scores in first and second grade classrooms. Results generally were consistent with those for the CLASS pre-K reported by Pianta et al. (2008) and Sandilos and DiPerna (2011). Specifically, estimates of internal consistency and inter-rater reliability (i.e., PWO and ICC) were high across all dimensions and domains. However, similar to the findings of Sandilos and DiPerna (2011) with the CLASS pre-K, estimates of CLASS K-3 score reliability were significantly lower when applying more stringent methods (i.e., exact agreement, Cohen's kappa, and linearly weighted kappa).

The current study also examined long-term stability utilizing two time points across an average of 10 months. Four dimensions (positive climate, behavior management, instructional learning formats, and quality feedback) and two domains (emotional support and classroom organization) yielded moderate long-term stability. The lower stability estimates observed for several dimensions might indicate that they are either more difficult to evaluate (e.g., concept development, language modeling) or that there are less opportunities for observers to witness examples of related behaviors (e.g., teacher sensitivity, regard for student perspectives). Lower long-term stability also could indicate that these facets of the classroom truly vary over time and/or in response to the student classroom population.

To date, no other studies have examined CLASS K-3 scores across academic years. Previous studies examined stability of CLASS K-3 scores within the same academic year (e.g., Pianta et al., 2008; Sandilos, 2012), and findings were generally consistent with the current study. However, only two CLASS K-3 domains (emotional support and classroom organization) and two dimensions (positive climate and behavior management) demonstrated moderate stability in both the current and previous studies (e.g., Pianta et al., 2008; Sandilos, 2012). Given that stability is an important consideration when utilizing scores formatively and evaluating change, further study is necessary to more fully understand the stability of dimensions and domains over varying time periods.

Limitations and Directions for Future Research

Several limitations should be considered when interpreting the results of the study. First, data were collected from two districts within one state, thus, the sample is not nationally representative. Future studies should sample classrooms representing various regions throughout the country (e.g., Northeast, Southeast,

Table 3:
Means, Standard Deviations, and Long-Term Stability Coefficients (ICCs) for CLASS K-3 Scores

Domain/dimension	Time 1 M (SD)	Time 2 M (SD)	ICC
Emotional support	4.76 (0.78)	4.83 (0.72)	.69*
Positive climate	5.20 (1.22)	5.03 (1.11)	.70*
Negative climate	2.95 (1.39)	2.50 (1.14)	.59*
Teacher sensitivity	4.64 (1.11)	4.52 (.95)	.33
Regard for student perspectives	3.55 (1.09)	3.95 (1.07)	.39
Classroom organization	5.27 (0.74)	5.32 (0.96)	.71*
Behavior management	5.70 (1.01)	5.80 (1.15)	.65*
Productivity	5.50 (0.91)	5.59 (1.21)	.33
Instructional learning formats	4.61 (0.86)	4.56 (0.97)	.71*
Instructional support	2.49 (1.01)	2.42 (0.99)	.53
Concept development	2.44 (1.08)	2.55 (1.25)	.21
Quality feedback	2.66 (1.17)	2.53 (1.26)	.66*
Language modeling	2.39 (1.08)	2.17 (0.89)	.33

*Note. ICCs calculated using 32-paired observations that were completed an average of 10 months apart. *p<.01.*

Midwest, Southwest, and Northwest). Another limitation of the current study is the relatively small number of raters. As scores on observational measures have the potential to be affected by observer characteristics, future studies should include larger numbers of observers and examine the impact of observer characteristics such as level of education, degree, and years of relevant experience.

In the current study, all observers had at least a bachelor's degree in psychology, education, or a related field; thus, there was not a large amount of variation. In addition, the current study only examined one version of the CLASS. As such, future research should examine reliability for the most recent additions to the CLASS system that are designed to measure upper elementary through high school as well as infancy. Finally, though establishing reliability is essential before using a measure in practice, of equal importance is establishing that score(s) measure the construct(s) of interest. As the current study only focused on score reliability, future studies should examine validity of CLASS K-3 scores.

Implications for Research and Practice

As a tool for collecting observational data in early education classrooms, the CLASS K-3 has several strengths. The CLASS framework is grounded in theory and relates to outcomes influence student's academic and social development (Hamre et al., 2009). Based on the results of the current study, CLASS K-3 scores demonstrate sufficient reliability for lower-stakes decisions, such as in formative evaluation. For example, CLASS K-3 observation data could be used to guide individualized feedback to teachers in an effort to create a targeted plan for professional development. However, given some of the reliability limitations highlighted by the more stringent indices reported in this study, CLASS users should heed the cautions of Stuhlman et al. (n.d.) regarding the use of specific cut scores to determine classroom proficiency. Instead, CLASS users should interpret scores in conjunction with other data from the classroom. In addition, observers should complete formal training as well as periodic booster sessions to maximize reliability of CLASS scores.

Author's Note

Correspondence concerning this article should be addressing to Molly Kaufman, 226 CEDAR Building, The Pennsylvania State University, University Park, PA, 16802. Email: msk268@psu.edu. The research reported here was supported by the Institute of Education Sciences, U.S. Department of Education, through Grant R305A090438 to The Pennsylvania State University. The opinions expressed are those of the authors and do not represent the views of the Institute or the U.S. Department of Education.

References

Brown, J. L., Jones, S. M., LaRusso, M. D., & Aber, J. L. (2010). Improving classroom quality: Teacher influences and experimental impacts of the 4Rs program. *Journal of Educational Psychology, 102*, 153-167. doi:10.1037/a0018160

Cadima, J., Leal, T., & Burchinal, M. (2010). The quality of teacher-student interactions: Associations with first graders' academic and behavioral outcomes. *The Journal of School Psychology, 48*, 457-482. doi:10.1016/j.jsp.2010.09.001

Curby, T. W., Rimm-Kaufman, S. E., & Ponitz, C. C. (2009). Teacher-child interactions and children's achievement trajectories across kindergarten and first grade. *Journal of Educational Psychology, 101*, 912-925. doi:10.1037/a0016647

Derrick-Mills, T., Burchinal, M., Peters, H.E., De Marco, A., Forestieri, N., Fyffe, S.,...Woods, T. (2016, September). *Early implementation of the Head Start designation renewal system: Volume I* (Research Report No. 2016-75a). Washington, DC: Office of Planning, Research and Evaluation, Administration for Children and Families, U.S. Department of Health and Human Services.

Early Childhood Learning & Knowledge Center (2014). *National CLASS Data 2014*. Retrieved from http://eclkc.ohs.acf.hhs.gov/hslc/data/class-reports/class-data-2014.html

Field, A. (2013). *Discovering statistics using IBM SPSS statistics*. London, England: SAGE.

Hadden, D. S., & Pianta, R. C. (2006). MyTeachingPartner: An innovative model of professional development. *YC Young Children, 61*(2), 42-43.

Hamre, B. K., Goffin, S. G., & Kraft-Sayre, M. (2009). *Classroom assessment scoring system implementation guide: Measuring and improving classroom interactions in early childhood settings.* Center for Advanced Study of Teaching and Learning. Retrieved from http://curry.virginia.edu/research/centers/castl/publications

Hamre, B. K., & Pianta, R. C. (2005). Can instructional and emotional support in the first-grade classroom make a difference for children at risk of school failure? *Child Development, 76,* 949-967. doi:10.1111/j.1467-8624.2005.00889.x

Howell, D. (2010). Intraclass correlation. In N. J. Salkind (Ed.), *Encyclopedia of Research Design* (pp. 637-642). Thousand Oaks, CA: SAGE. doi: http://dx.doi.org/10.4135/9781412961288.n198

Makel, M. C., & Plucker, J. A. (2014). Facts are more important than novelty: Replication in the education sciences. *Educational Researcher, 43*(6), 304-316.

Pianta, R., Downer, J., & Hamre, B. (2016). Quality in early education classrooms: Definitions, gaps, and systems. *The Future of Children, 26*(2), 119-137. doi:10.1353/foc.2016.0015

Pianta, R., La Paro, K., & Hamre, B. (2008). *Classroom Assessment Scoring System (CLASS) Manual, K-3.* Baltimore, MD: Paul H. Brookes.

Plank, S. B., & Condliffe, B. F. (2013) Pressures of the season: An examination of classroom quality and high-stakes accountability. *American Educational Research Journal, 50,* 1152-1182. doi:10.3102/0002831213500691

Sandilos, L. E. (2012). *Measuring quality in rural kindergarten classrooms: Reliability and validity evidence for the classroom assessment scoring system, kindergarten–third grade (CLASS K-3)* (Doctoral dissertation). Retrieved from https://etda.libraries.psu.edu/

Sandilos, L. E., & DiPerna, J. C. (2011). Interrater reliability of the Classroom Assessment Scoring System—pre-K. *Journal of Early Childhood and Infant Psychology, 7,* 65-84. Retrieved from http://www.pace.edu/press/journals/journal-of-early-childhood-and-infant-psychology

Stuhlman, M. W., Hamre, B. K., Downer, J. T., & Pianta, R. C. (n.d.). *How to use classroom observation most effectively* [Pamphlet]. Center for Advanced Study of Teaching and Learning. Retrieved November 16, 2016 from http://curry.virginia.edu/uploads/resourceLibrary/CASTL_practioner_Part4_single

Contributors

James C. DiPerna, Ph.D., is Professor in the School Psychology Program at The Pennsylvania State University. His research focuses on assessment and intervention strategies to promote students' social, emotional, and academic success.

Molly S. Kaufman is a doctoral candidate in the school psychology program at the Pennsylvania State University, where she received her M.Ed. in 2015. She currently serves as a graduate assistant at the Clearinghouse for Military Family Readiness. At the Clearinghouse, she engages in implementation science, program evaluation, and outreach to advance the health and well-being of military families.

Perspectives on
Early Childhood Psychology and Education

PECPE publishes twice a year, in the fall and spring. These two special issues on specific topics are edited by one of the journal's associate editors, and also include a few general articles.

Editorial Policy and Submission Guidelines

Perspectives on Early Childhood Psychology and Education focuses on publishing original contributions from a broad range of psychological and educational perspectives relevant to infants, young children (to age 8 years), families, and caregivers. Manuscripts incorporating evidence-based research, theory, and practice within clinical, community, developmental, neurological, and school psychology perspectives are considered. In addition, the journal accepts test and book reviews, literature reviews, program descriptions and evaluations, clinical studies, and other professional materials of interest to psychologists and educators working with young children. Proposals for special focus topics may be made to the Editor.

Format: Manuscripts should be original work not currently submitted for publication to other journals. Authors must follow the guidelines of the Publication Manual of the American Psychological Association (Sixth Edition). Manuscripts may not exceed 35 double-spaced pages in length, including the cover page, abstract, references, tables and figures.

Submission: Submit an electronic copy of the manuscript for editorial review. Avoid including any identifying author information in the text. Selection of manuscripts is based on blind peer review. Include a cover page with the following information: the title of article, author(s) full name(s), title(s), institution or professional affiliations, and mailing and email address of primary author.

The cover page will not be sent to reviewers.

Selection Criteria:

• Importance of topic in early childhood psychology
  and education

• Theory and research related to content

• Contribution to professional practice in early childhood
  psychology and education

• Clear and concise writing

Submit manuscripts to the Editor at the following address:

Dr. Vincent C. Alfonso
Gonzaga University
School of Education
502 East Boone Avenue
Spokane, WA 99258

Email: PECPE@gonzaga.edu

CALL FOR PAPERS

Special Focus:
Gender diversity: nonconformity and fostering acceptance

While there is evidence of greater acceptance of gender diversity, educators, psychologists, and parents must often address the challenges presented by young children who do not conform to typical gender roles. There is much to learn about young children at odds with prevailing gender identity and expression norms. This special focus of *Perspectives on Early Childhood Psychology and Education* (PECPE) invites manuscripts that explore young children's understanding of gender; resilience and risk factors, as well as eventual outcomes of early gender nonconformity. Since outcomes are often influenced by the responses of others, manuscripts can also address peer or adult attitudes and behaviors related to young children who resist or comply with gender norms, and innovative programs and strategies to create healthy and affirming environments that support nonconforming youngsters.

Manuscripts should be original work not currently submitted for publication to other journals. Authors must follow the guidelines of the *Publication Manual of the American Psychological Association* (Sixth Edition). Manuscripts may not exceed 35 double-spaced pages in length, including the cover page, abstract, references, tables, and figures. Avoid including any identifying author information in the text. Selection of manuscripts is based on blind peer review. Include a cover page with the following information: the title of article, author(s) full name(s), title(s), institution or professional affiliations, and mailing and email address of primary author. The cover page will not be sent to reviewers.

Submit an electronic copy of special focus manuscripts for editorial review to Dr. Florence Rubinson, Associate Editor, PECPE, Rubinson@brooklyn.cuny.edu by **August 15, 2017**.

General manuscripts for PECPE should follow the same format and submission guidelines except that they should be sent to Dr. Vincent C. Alfonso, Editor, PECPE: PECPE@gonzaga.edu or alfonso@gonzaga.edu by **August 15, 2017**.

Volume 2, Issue 1 of
Perspectives on Early Childhood Psychology and Education
was published in Spring 2017
by Pace University Press

Cover and Interior Design by Sara Yager
Cover and Interior Layout by Taylor Lear
The journal was typeset in Minion and Myriad
and printed by Lightning Source in La Vergne, Tennessee

Pace University Press

Director: Sherman Raskin
Associate Director: Manuela Soares
Marketing Manager: Patricia Hinds
Design Consultant: Sara Yager

Graduate Assistants: Taylor Lear and Rachel Diebel
Student Aide: Kelsey O'Brien-Enders

www.ingramcontent.com/pod-product-compliance
Lightning Source LLC
Chambersburg PA
CBHW061018280326
41935CB00009B/1014